Donald. A. Lowle

D0177821

the *cat*
IN
ANCIENT
EGYPT

the *cat*
IN
ANCIENT
EGYPT

Jaromir Malek

Published by British Museum Press
for the Trustees
of the British Museum

To Jane, for patience.
To Pandora, for being herself.
To those fighting against the trade
in animal furs, for courage.

© 1993 Jaromir Malek

Published by British Museum Press
A division of British Museum Publications Ltd
46 Bloomsbury Street, London WC1B 3QQ

British Library Cataloguing in Publication Data
A catalogue record for this book is available
from the British Library

ISBN 0 7141 0969 X

Designed by James Shurmer

Jacket designed by Grahame Dudley Associates

Typeset by Rowland Phototypesetting Ltd
Bury St Edmunds, Suffolk

Printed in Great Britain by
Butler & Tanner Ltd, Frome and London

(*Front cover*) The Egyptian cat, after MS Egypt a 4 (P)
section A/4, Bodleian Library, University of Oxford.

(*Back cover*) Three bronze statuettes from the British
Museum Collection. From left: BM 47547, BM 64391,
BM 58517.

(*Frontispiece*) The ancient Egyptian cat: sleek, elegant, and
with an aura of aloofness and mystery. No other animal
better conjures up the image of pharaonic civilization.
British Museum.

Contents

'For he is hated by the hypocrite and miser.
For the former is affraid of detection.
For the latter refuses the charge.'
(Christopher Smart, *Jubilate Agno*, 1760)

Acknowledgements

I wish to thank Carolyn Jones for editing the text of
this book, her cat Domino for taking an active part in
assembling its illustrations, and James Shurmer for
designing it; their contribution goes far beyond this
brief mention. I am also grateful to my friends in the
Department of Egyptian Antiquities of the British
Museum, in particular Carol Andrews, Stephen
Quirke, and John Taylor, for their help. While I was
enjoying myself, they gave of their precious time
generously and ungrudgingly. The Keeper of
Egyptian Antiquities, Mr W. V. Davies, kindly
allowed me to study and illustrate many previously
unpublished objects.

A note on Egyptian words:

As the precise vocalization of most Egyptian words is
uncertain, they are given in a modified Egyptological
transliteration. This may be something of a make-
believe, but has the merit of allowing us to pronounce
them.

Chronological chart

BC	ANCIENT EGYPT
*c.*5000–3000	Predynastic Period
*c.*3000–2950	'Dynasty O'
	Narmer
*c.*2950–2647	The Early Dynastic Period
	First Dynasty
	Second Dynasty
	Hotepsekhemwy
2647–2124	The Old Kingdom (Third to Eighth Dynasties)
2647–2573	Third Dynasty
2573–2454	Fourth Dynasty
2549–2526	Khufu
2518–2493	Khafra
2488–2460	Menkaura
2454–2311	Fifth Dynasty
2447–2435	Sahura
2408–2377	Nyuserra
2311–2140	Sixth Dynasty
2311–2281	Teti
2280–2243	Pepy I
2236–2143	Pepy II
2140–2134	Seventh Dynasty
2134–2124	Eighth Dynasty

2123–*c*.2040	The First Intermediate Period (Ninth to mid-Eleventh Dynasties)
2123–2040	Ninth/Tenth (Heracleopolitan) Dynasty
2123–*c*.2040	Eleventh (Theban) Dynasty (*1st part*)
2050–*c*.2040	Mentuhotep II (*before re-unification*)
c.2040–1648	The Middle Kingdom (mid-Eleventh to Thirteenth Dynasties)
c.2040–1980	Eleventh (Theban) Dynasty (*2nd part*)
c.2040–1999	Mentuhotep II (*after re-unification*)
1980–1801	Twelfth Dynasty
1980–1951	Amenemhat I
1960–1916	Senusret I
1918–1884	Amenemhat II
1886–1878	Senusret II
1878–1859	Senusret III
1859–1814	Amenemhat III
1814–1805	Amenemhat IV
1805–1801	Sobekneferu (Queen)
1801–1648	Thirteenth Dynasty
1648–1540	The Second Intermediate Period (Fourteenth to Seventeenth Dynasties)
1648–1540	Fourteenth, Fifteenth ('The Hyksos') and Sixteenth ('The Lesser Hyksos') Dynasties (contemporary)
1648–1550	Seventeenth (Theban) Dynasty
	Intef V
	Seqenenra Taa II
	(plus *c*. the first decade of the reign of Ahmose I of the Eighteenth Dynasty)

1540–1196	The New Kingdom (Eighteenth to Twentieth Dynasties)	
1540 (1550)–1296	Eighteenth Dynasty	
1540 (accession 1550)–1525		Ahmose I
1525–1504		Amenhotep I
1504–1492		Thutmose I
1492–1479		Thutmose II
1479–1457		Hatshepsut (Queen)
1479–1425		Thutmose III
1427–1401		Amenhotep II
1401–1391		Thutmose IV
1391–1353		Amenhotep III
1353–1337		Amenhotep IV = Akhenaten
1338–1336		Smenkhkare
1336–1327		Tutankhamun
1327–1323		Ay
1323–1295		Horemheb
1295–1186	Nineteenth Dynasty	
1295–1294		Ramses I
1294–1279		Sety I
1279–1213		Ramses II
1213–1203		Merenptah
1203–1200		Amenmessu
1200–1194		Sety II
1194–1188		Saptah
1188–1186		Tausret (Queen)
1186–1069	Twentieth Dynasty	
1184–1153		Ramses III
1153–1147		Ramses IV

9

1069–c.715	The Third Intermediate Period (Twenty-first to Twenty-fourth Dynasties)
1069–945	Twenty-first Dynasty
945–715	Twenty-second Dynasty
924–889	Osorkon I
874–850	Osorkon II
773–767	Pamiu
818–715	Twenty-third Dynasty
727–715	Twenty-fourth Dynasty
c.715–343	The Late Period (Twenty-fifth to Thirtieth Dynasties and the 'Second Persian Period')
c.715–656	Twenty-fifth (Nubian) Dynasty
716–702	Shabako
664–525	Twenty-sixth (Saite) Dynasty
664–610	Psamtek I
610–595	Nekau II
595–589	Psamtek II
589–570	Apries
570–526	Ahmose
526–525	Psamtek III
525–404	Twenty-seventh (Persian) Dynasty
525–522	Cambyses
404–399	Twenty-eighth Dynasty
399–380	Twenty-ninth Dynasty
380–343	Thirtieth Dynasty
360–342	Nectanebo II
342–332	The 'Second Persian Period'

BC	GRECO-ROMAN EGYPT
332–305	Macedonian Dynasty
332	Alexander the Great conquers Egypt
305–30	Ptolemaic Dynasty
30 BC–AD 395	Roman province
AD 395–642	Byzantine Egypt
	ISLAMIC EGYPT
639–642	Arabs, led by Amr ibn al-As, conquer Egypt

Note on the chronological scheme for ancient Egypt:
The dates may be regarded as certain for the Late Period. The possible margin of error should not exceed fifteen years for the New Kingdom, some forty years for the Middle Kingdom, sixty years for the Old Kingdom, and about 100 years for the first two dynasties.

1 (*Above*) and 2 (*Right*) The bronze 'Gayer-Anderson cat,' *c*.664–30 BC, probably the most spectacular among the many thousands of such statuettes, is anatomically startlingly well observed and finely decorated with silver inlays and gold earrings and a nose-ring. It is known by the name of the collector who presented it to the British Museum. See also the frontispiece.

3 (*Far right*) Nowadays Egyptian cats display a much greater variety of colours and coat-patterns than their ancestors but, as far as one can judge from ancient Egyptian evidence, their behaviour has changed little.

Prologue

The modern Egyptian domestic cat, which one encounters in the cafes and bazaars, in the noisy streets of Cairo and in the dusty sun-drenched villages, is a graceful and delicate little creature, usually much smaller than Western cats. The intensity of its attentive gaze is unnerving and almost tangible; the speed of its lightning reactions makes you gasp. It is hard to believe that the ancestors of this entertaining but humble animal played such an important part in everyday life in ancient Egypt.

Where did it all begin? One of the closest wild relatives of the modern cat was *Felis silvestris libyca*, or the African wild cat, with tawny, yellow-grey fur and striped markings which provided ideal camouflage among the rocks and sand of the desert. This was a larger beast than the little cats of today: a predator rather than a scavenger. Occasionally, among the multi-coloured cats of modern Egypt, one can still see an animal that seems to revert to its ancient ancestry. Several years ago I saw such a one climbing the Great Pyramid of King Khufu (2549–2526 BC) at Giza – an animal with superb yellow and cream fur, brindled with fine lines of silvery grey. It is strictly

forbidden to climb the pyramids, but this prohibition cannot, of course, be enforced on cats, and the cat was making its way upwards, safe from all human interference, its coat blending perfectly with the rugged texture of the ancient stones. No doubt, there would be plenty of prey on the pyramid, in the shape of careless birds, and perhaps small creatures such as lizards. In the suffocating heat and the blinding sun the cat calmly went about its own private concerns, high above the mass of humanity milling about below and with total disregard for their incomprehensible trivial pursuits.

There are innumerable ways of approaching ancient civilizations, although I suspect that those who suggest that we can ever understand them fully are deluding themselves. The traditional well-tried methods concentrate, in a broad sweep, on the fluctuating fortunes of the kings and their courts, the rise and fall of empires, and the monuments of the mighty. But a large canvas and a thick brush dilute rather than focus attention, and tend to stress the unusual, the strange, and the heroic, making communication between now and then difficult. The unexceptional, the normal, and the ordinary – and this, like it or not, applies to most of us – usually remains unspoken. Yet recognition and familiarity are the elder sisters of understanding. The ancient Egyptian domestic cat was the ancestor of many of our cats. Our modern cat represents one of the few remaining links between the ancient Egyptian civilization and the completely different world of today. The animal has remained essentially the same (or so at least it seems from the surviving evidence), and our attitudes, feelings and prejudices towards cats, and animals in general, can be directly compared with those of the ancient Egyptians. Are we really that much different, in spite of the time, geography, language, and technology? And if so, are we better people?

4 The modern Egyptian cat: just like its ancient ancestors, it is street-wise and alert, always on the look-out for advantageous opportunities which might present themselves.

Running free
The wild cats

A revolutionary change in the lifestyle of people who traversed and inter-mittently inhabited the north-eastern corner of the African continent took place shortly before 4000 BC. It was then that the first permanent settlements of sun-dried mud-brick houses began to appear along the river Nile. Initially, they were mainly situated on higher ground at the foot of the rising *gebel* (desert plateau) along the narrow river valley and on the 'turtle-backs,' the sandy ridges in the flat expanse of the northern delta, which afforded some protection against unexpectedly high floods. Roving cattle-breeders, peripatetic plant-gatherers and seasonal cultivators were becoming settled farmers. These were the first steps towards the future splendour of the pharaonic cities, but also towards one of the most ambiguous and volatile relationships the animal world and humankind have ever known, that of cats and people.

The dependence of the early societies on favourable geographic and climatic factors was almost absolute. Their combination in predynastic Egypt (before *c.*3000 BC) was uniquely suited to farming and animal husbandry. Rain played almost no part in the country's climate, but every year around 19 July (of the Julian calendar), when the star Sopdet (Sirius) reappeared on the morning horizon after a prolonged period of invisibility, it heralded the imminent arrival of the annual flood and the beginning of a new calendar year. The Nile, which was, and still is, the main geographical and ecological feature of the area, rose swiftly. The Egyptians referred to it simply as *iteru,* 'river,' but the waters of the inundation were personified under the name Hapy. According to a text known as *The Hymn to Hapy*, 'when he appears, the land jubilates, everybody rejoices, every jawbone puts on a smile, every tooth is bared.' The river remained swollen until September and during this period much of the valley and the delta was under several feet of water. All agricultural activities ceased, and many villages became temporary islands hardly showing above the waters of this annually-recurring deluge. When at last the inundation receded, it left behind a deposit of rich organic silt, mostly a decaying vegetable matter, which restored the land's fertility. Large shallow pools of stagnant muddy water dotted the river banks for some time. Before they dried up under the scorching sun, they provided enough water for plants which were sown in their immediate vicinity, and the early settlers soon learnt to make it last even longer by constructing simple dykes and canals. Farming

5 The counting of cattle paraded in groups of five, on a wall-painting from the Theban tomb of Nebamun, *c.*1450 BC or a little later. British Museum.

and cattle-breeding were accompanied by progress in crafts and the production of modest artistic creations which can be easily followed in surviving evidence. However, spiritual development is much more elusive and difficult to trace, and in the absence of any written sources we must rely on its often incomplete reflection in the mirror of archaeological artefacts.

Advances in material culture went hand in hand with the fast-growing social stratification of Egyptian society. This can be detected in the increasing differences in the number and quality of goods which accompanied the dead into the next world, and the size and degree of elaboration in the construction of tombs and graves. At first, the privileged individuals buried in these tombs were almost certainly chiefs and elders of village communities and their families. Differences in local conditions (which favoured some areas more than others), the growing personal ambitions and expectations of community leaders and the ease of communications along the Nile, eventually led to the formation of larger social units. Geographically, Egypt was naturally delimited by the deserts in the east-west direction. Impenetrable marshy areas and the shore of the Mediterranean formed the country's northern

6 The stocktaking of geese, and putting them in crates, shown on a wall-painting from the Theban tomb of Nebamun, probably *c*.1450 or a little later. British Museum.

boundary. The granite barrier of the first Nile cataract at Aswan presented a formidable obstacle to river navigation in the south and separated Egypt from Nubia. Before long the ethnically varied settlers in the northern reaches of the Nile valley became the most advanced nation in the area, leaving their nomadic neighbours far behind. Shortly after 3000 BC, there emerged in Egypt a unified state governed by one ruler. Rudimentary hieroglyphs appeared at about the same time; Egypt crossed the line separating prehistory and history. The period between *c*.3000 BC and the conquest of Egypt by Alexander the Great in 332 BC represents the flowering of Egyptian 'dynastic' (a reference to the Egyptian royal houses or 'dynasties') or pharaonic civilization.

Egypt proper (*Kemi*, 'Black Land') consisted of two geographically different parts which were in many respects diametrical opposites. A narrow stretch of fertile land along the Nile in southern (or Middle and Upper) Egypt was known as *Ta-shema*, from the words *ta*, 'land,' and *shema*, 'narrow,' while the broad flat delta in the north (Lower Egypt) was *Ta-mehu*, from the word *meh*, 'to fill.' Vast, inhospitable deserts (not considered part of *Kemi*) stretched

7 In southern Egypt, the Nile valley is often little more than a blue ribbon of river bordered by narrow strips of fertile land.

on either side of the river to the east and west. Egyptian fauna and flora reflected this division. On the whole, the Egyptian animal world was remarkably benign. It presented only limited dangers to humans and could be easily exploited by them.

The Nile was the giver of life and the main traffic artery, and its marshes and muddy shores were the habitat of many animals and birds. The river was teeming with fish, but these were regarded as ritually impure, forbidden to priests on duty, and were absent from the lists of food offerings in the tombs of the priests and officials. This concept, which seems so strange in a country completely dominated by a river, probably originated among the nomadic people who contributed significantly to the population of predynastic Egypt. Nevertheless, fish was the staple diet of ordinary peasants and craftsmen. The river also harboured the crocodile, by far the greatest threat to people and their livestock. Tomb reliefs often depict these beasts lurking in the water while herdsmen, trusting the efficacy of their magical spells, cross a canal in small papyrus skiffs followed by their cattle. Crocodiles remained numerous in all parts of Egypt well into the late Middle Ages. In our own century they could still be seen in the area south of the first Nile cataract at Aswan, and I recall vividly encounters with these animals near Sayyala and Korosko during the UNESCO campaign to save the monuments of Nubia in the mid-1960s. There are reports that the shores of Lake Nasser have now provided the crocodile with new breeding grounds and that their numbers are again on the increase.

The most powerful animal living in the Nile was the hippopotamus, frequently met in Egypt during the third millennium BC, but gradually declining from about 1500 BC and finally becoming extinct in the early nineteenth century AD. In pharaonic Egypt, the mighty hippopotamus was hunted mainly as an undesirable animal which destroyed crops and wreaked havoc in cultivated fields.

8 Spectacularly patterned sand dunes can form in the Western (Libyan) Desert; the Eastern Desert is more a rocky wilderness.

9 A hippopotamus hunt in the marshes shown on a painted relief in the tomb-chapel of the vizier Mereruka at Saqqara, *c.*2300 BC.

The dense and steamily humid marshes were at first widespread but as agriculture intensified and the population increased, they came to be confined to certain areas, notably the delta. They were the home for an astonishing variety of birds. Just listing their names conjures up the image of this bird paradise, where tall rushes sway gently over the quiet water: cormorant, heron, egret, ibis, flamingo, shelduck, teal, lapwing, sandpiper, plover, avocet, kingfisher, stork, hoopoe, and many others. On the reliefs and paintings in Egyptian tombs, birds are often depicted rising like a thick cloud from a papyrus thicket when disturbed by the flight of a hunter's throwstick or by the stealthy approach of a marauding predator, such as the ichneumon, the genet, or the cat. The hieroglyphic script contains at least thirty signs which are ornithologically-accurate images of birds, and a detailed palaeographic study of these hieroglyphs would almost certainly identify more.

Beyond the fertile green valley and the delta there stretched the deserts. The Egyptians recognized from the earliest times the necessity of venturing into these inhospitable regions in search of valuable metals and much needed

10 A papyrus marsh teeming with birds, on a relief, originally painted, from the cult-temple of King Userkaf (2454–2447 BC) at Saqqara. Cairo, Egyptian Museum.

minerals or in order to procure luxury goods, not available in their own country, by long-distance trading. On the whole, however, the deserts were the equivalent of 'abroad,' areas inhabited by unfriendly people speaking strange tongues, the home of weird creatures and mythical beasts, and so they were intensely disliked and feared. To die abroad threatened one's chances of life after death. Ancient Egyptians were profoundly home-oriented, and in this respect modern Egyptians are not much different. It was not until the second half of the third century AD that some of the descendants of ancient Egyptians, the persecuted Christian Copts, voluntarily withdrew into the wilderness of the deserts in order to lead the life of hermits. Areas closer to the river, especially along *wadis* (desert valleys), were not entirely barren but resembled savannas rather than deserts. They supported limited vegetation and provided the habitat for a variety of wildlife.

The environment was profoundly influenced not only by advancing aridity but by man's activities, such as hunting and cattle-grazing. In pharaonic Egypt hunting no longer played a significant part in the country's economy. There were professional hunters who, at least during the third millennium BC, procured animals to be offered in tombs and temples or to be kept for breeding. These had to be captured alive and this explains the seemingly laborious method of lassoing animals such as ibexes, represented on the walls of Old-Kingdom (2647–2124 BC) tombs. The king and his officials also indulged in the killing of animals as a sport, and archery skills were much vaunted. The ibex, oryx and several species of gazelle and antelope, but also the wild bull and the lion, were the main animals hunted. Limited and unsuccessful attempts were also made to domesticate some of them. Herds of big game, such as the elephant and the giraffe, had been recorded in a remarkably realistic fashion in prehistoric rock-drawings, but they retreated south into Upper Nubia (beyond the second Nile cataract and further south, modern Sudan) well before the beginning of the pharaonic era. The lion roamed the margins of the Egyptian deserts at all times. There were also wolves, jackals, hyenas and caracals. The ostrich gradually became a rare visitor, and its feathers and eggs were imported as precious commodities from Nubia. Ostriches in any significant numbers were last seen in Egyptian deserts in the nineteenth century AD although there are occasional reports of more recent sightings.

Zoologically, small cats (genus *Felis*) are mammals and carnivores which belong to the family *Felidae* (this also contains three species of *Lynx*, the large cats, and the cheetah) but their classification is by no means universally agreed on. The swamp or jungle cat (*Felis chaus*) and the African wild cat (*Felis silvestris libyca*) are the two wild species encountered in Egypt. Their presence is confirmed by many reports and observations made in the past two hundred years, particularly since the French invasion under Napoleon in 1798 and Muhammad Ali's reforms in the first half of the nineteenth century which made Egypt more accessible to European travellers and naturalists.

The swamp or jungle cat, *Felis chaus*, is the larger and heavier of the two indigenous wild cats. Its specialist Latin name derives, etymologically inaccurately, from the Coptic *shau*, 'tomcat,' but there is at least some justification in using an Egyptian word because this cat does not occur elsewhere on the African continent (although it is found further east, as far as south-eastern Asia). As its popular name suggests, it prefers marshy areas with dense ground cover. In modern times it has been seen only in the delta and the northern part of the Nile valley, but the situation would have been different in ancient

11 The swamp cat (*Felis chaus*), the larger and heavier of the two indigenous species of small cats known from Egypt.

12 The African wild cat (*Felis silvestris libyca*), a close relative of ancient Egyptian domesticated cats and a distant ancestor of many of our cats.

times. The combined head and body length of the swamp cat is *c*.650–750mm,
with long legs but – an important characteristic – a relatively short tail, *c*.250–
300mm. Its ears are long and tufted. These cats weigh on average between
3.5 and 6.5kg (8–14lbs). They are usually plain-coloured without distinctive
body markings, ranging from light reddish brown or sandy fawn to grey, with
black-tipped ears and tail, and with faint stripes on the head, a darker dorsal
line and stripes on the upper legs and the tail.

The African wild cat (*Felis silvestris libyca*, also *Felis maniculata*) is very adept
at adjusting to varying surroundings. It is much more lightly built than *Felis
chaus*. Its head and body length is *c*.600mm which makes the tail, measuring
c.350mm, proportionally long. The ears are not tufted. The legs are long
when compared with modern cats. The body colour can vary considerably
according to the habitat but the markings of the fur, which are not unlike
those of our striped tabby, are an important feature. Pale sandy fawn is the
most common colour, with a rufous line on the back and multiple transverse

stripes of the same colour, though paler, on the body. These may also appear on the head and usually extend to the legs. The black-tipped tail is ringed.

The overall area of Egypt is $c.1,000.000\text{km}^2$, but only some $40,000\text{km}^2$ is cultivable land; the rest is desert. In all countries where natural resources have to be used in a very intensive way, fauna and flora are affected profoundly through the elimination of unwanted dangerous or damaging species, over-exploitation of others, and the introduction of new varieties. The fauna and flora of ancient Egypt were quite different from those of today and many plants and animals now firmly associated with the popular image of the country were either unknown in antiquity or were introduced relatively late – it will suffice to mention the horse, camel, water buffalo, turkey and chicken, and sugar cane, cotton, oranges, bananas, and potatoes. It is, therefore, necessary to establish whether the situation concerning the small cats was the same in ancient Egypt as in more modern times. The evidence which we shall examine is that of the Egyptian language, the skeletal remains, especially those of mummified cats, and art, in particular representations in tomb wall-paintings and reliefs.

The Egyptians were always rather inclined to rigid categorization. Their custom of listing items according to formal criteria, such as materials, was the result of a long scribal and bureaucratic tradition and can be a source of invaluable information, but also of much frustration, for modern scholars. Written sources, however, do not offer us much assistance here. The Egyptians did not distinguish lexicographically between different wild cats, nor did they differentiate between wild and domesticated cats. There was only one word for the cat in pharaonic Egyptian which we can find in the hieroglyphic writing. It was the onomatopoeic *miu* or *mii* (feminine *miit*), *imi* (feminine *imiit* or *miat*) in demotic, the penultimate stage of the Egyptian language, and *emu* or *amu* in Coptic, written from *c.* the third century AD. The cat was simply '(s)he who mews,' and as we shall see, this was how the Egyptians themselves understood it. The word described the whole genus, *Felis*, and could also be applied to one or two other animals similar in appearance.

The Bohairic and Fayumic (Lower Egyptian) dialects of Coptic used the word *shau* or *djeu*, of unclear etymology, in order to refer to a male cat. The Greek *gale*, 'ferret,' 'weasel,' became Coptic *kle*, with the meaning 'cat,' perhaps more as a reference to the comparable usefulness of the animal rather than any other similarity – the Greeks and Romans kept ferrets in order to rid their houses and barns of vermin. Even the Arabic *hirr* (feminine *hirra*) could exceptionally be adopted into Coptic as *her*, but all these were late additions made well after the eclipse of the pharaonic civilization. The situation is rather surprising when compared with the variety of words for the dog, but it is consistent with other known facts, such as the large number of proper names for dogs, and their almost complete absence for cats.

Attempts at identifying mummified cats (most of these date to the first millennium BC, relatively late in pharaonic Egypt) have in the past produced curiously differing and (for a non-specialist) confusing results, much influenced by the strongly-felt need to distinguish between wild/semi-wild and domesticated cats. It seems reasonable to expect that the majority of mummified cats were domesticated animals which came either from temple catteries or from ordinary households. It is, then, puzzling to observe that many of them are larger than the modern wild *Felis silvestris libyca* (normally domesticated animals are smaller). Osteological (skeletal) differences may, however, be too small and the variations within each group too wide (not to mention the differences in the size of males and females) to provide reliable information on the animal's status.

Furthermore, in ancient Egypt contacts between domesticated and wild cats and the ensuing hybridization would have been unavoidable. There must have been semi-domesticated and feral cats and dogs roaming Egyptian towns and villages, but also wild animals would have strayed into settlements from time to time. In a demotic story of Setne Khaemwaset, dating to the Ptolemaic period (after 332 BC), the protagonist dreams of becoming so infatuated with

13 The serval (*Felis serval*), on a fragment of a faience plaque of the reign of Thutmose III (1492–1425 BC), from the temple of the goddess Hathor at Serabit el-Khadim in the Sinai. British Museum.

14 Nubian princes bringing tribute, including skins of the serval or civet cat. A wall-painting in the tomb of Huy, the Nubian viceroy of Tutankhamun (1336–1327 BC).

Tabubu, the daughter of the prophet of the goddess Bastet, that he agrees when she suggests that his children should be killed and their bodies thrown out of the window to be devoured by cats and dogs. Fortunately, this was just a bad dream described in a work of fiction though it probably reflected reality in that scavenging animals, including cats, were a common sight.

The mummies of cats are invaluable in order to establish which species of cats were known in antiquity, but as a rule they do not shed sufficient light on whether these animals were wild, tame or domesticated. It seems that they can be safely divided only between *Felis silvestris libyca* (a vast majority, no doubt mostly domesticated cats) and *Felis chaus* (only a few in each of the groups examined, perhaps tamed or wild cats).

A few specimens of the serval (*Felis serval*) also appear to have been identified among cat mummies, but it is not clear whether the serval has ever been indigenous to Egypt. These animals may have been regarded as exotic cats and imported from the south; cats (*mii*) of Miu, a locality in Nubia, are mentioned in a Ramesside (1295–1069 BC) list of Nubian tribute. Many faience plaques found in the temple of Hathor at Serabit el-Khadim, in southern Sinai, bear representations of the serval. Some of them are accompanied by the cartouches of Queen Hatshepsut (1479–1457 BC) and Thutmose III (1492–1425 BC). The animals were sketched before the plaques were glazed and display the typically strong spotted pattern of the serval's coat, with its whiskers prominently marked. The pelts of small animals which, it has been suggested, might be those of the serval or civet cat (*Viverra civetta*) are shown as part of the tribute of Nubia in the Theban tomb (TT 40) of the viceroy of Kush, Amenhotep Huy, of the reign of Tutankhamun (1336–1327 BC).

No certain representations of the civet cat are known from Egypt. Animals and animal products were always an important element of tribute and war booty: bears from Western Asia are depicted in the pyramid-complex of King Sahura (2447–2435 BC) at Abusir, but in later times most of the exotic fauna came from the south, e.g. monkeys and baboons, giraffes, ostriches, and cheetahs.

It is rather ironic, but illustrates well the difficulties experienced by those who study ancient Egyptian civilization, that what could be the earliest representations of small wild cats are so uncertain as to be virtually excluded from serious consideration. They occur in the largest and most comprehensive wildlife scene known from the third millennium BC. This was found broken up into hundreds of small fragments in the sun-temple of King Nyuserra (2408–2377 BC) at Abu Gurab, on the west bank of the Nile south-west of Cairo. Around 2450 BC, the cult of the sun-god Ra (or Atum) of On (Heliopolis, nowadays a north-eastern suburb of Cairo) became so important that for the next hundred years each king built for him a special temple in the vicinity of the state capital, Inebhedj, 'White Wall' (later Memphis). The king was now described as 'the son of the god Ra.' The sun-temples were architecturally unusual buildings and the focal point of each was an obelisk (a tall structure resembling a massive column of a rectangular plan, tapering towards the summit), the symbol of the sun-god. In the sun-temple of Nyuserra, a long corridor which started at the main entrance and approached the obelisk by skirting a large court open to the sun, eventually led to a chamber named by Egyptologists the 'Room of the Seasons.' On its walls there were representations of the Egyptian countryside which illustrated the life-giving qualities of the sun-god. They were arranged according to the three seasons of the Egyptian calendar year: *akhet* (inundation), *peret* (winter), and *shemu* (summer).

Cats appear several times. One fragment shows two registers (horizontal bands into which the available space on the wall was divided) of incompletely preserved animals, including a hound, antelope, oryx, and a cat. The cat has a remarkably long tail and appears to be too large for *Felis silvestris libyca*, but the relative sizes of representations were subject to special rules in Egyptian art and are not always a reliable guide. The colour of the coat of the animal was not preserved and the fragment, which the archaeologists brought home to Germany, was destroyed during the Second World War; therefore, the accuracy of the available copy cannot be checked. Several other fragmentary reliefs from Abu Gurab are equally uncertain.

Animals in ancient Egyptian art are usually remarkably well-observed and accurately portrayed. The manner in which they were depicted was less dependent on the 'canonized' image than representations of human figures, and they are more easily comprehensible to those untrained in the unusual conventions which govern these images. Casual sketches of animals made on ostraca (flakes of limestone) during the Ramesside period (1295–1069 BC) show that when freed from the constrictions of formality, some Egyptian draughtsmen, like all great artists, were able to convey the character of an animal in a few deft touches of the brush.

Egyptian art was anything but art for art's sake, and should not be approached uncritically. Superficially examined, scenes shown in the tombs of wealthy Egyptians may give the impression of being a spontaneous and faithful reflection of reality, with a mass of convincing detail. We must not, however, forget that they were intended to be functional rather than decorative, and that they played an important and well-defined role in the ideological (religious) context of the tomb. The reality which these scenes portray is the wished-for reality of the life beyond the grave, carefully selected, censored, proven by use, and deeply rooted in religious and artistic traditions, combined with a host of traditional and symbolic allusions and visual references.

At first, from about 2650 BC, tomb representations were mainly preoccupied with the material provisioning of the tomb which was essential for the continued existence of the tomb owner (or, to be more precise, one of his 'modes of existence,' his *ka*) after death. Activities portrayed there were an extension of the early pictorial lists of food and drink offerings. Such offerings brought to the tomb by the deceased's relatives or by the priests contracted to look after the tomb could be substituted, it was thought, by their representations or conjured-up by the recitation of prescribed spells. The logic of this was impeccable: there was never any attempt to pretend that the tomb owner's *ka* required more than the spiritual substance of the offered food, and when the offerings were removed from the altar or table they were consumed by the priests and their families. This remarkably 'realistic' way of looking at the presentation of offerings to the dead avoided waste (with only a few exceptions, foodstuffs were not made unconsumable in the process) and the 'spiritual substitution' avoided excesses. In a country which, to our eyes, was obsessed with the service of the dead, presentation of offerings never reached the point when it would have represented an intolerable drain on Egyptian economy. In fact, it is possible to visualize an economic system developing in which, ultimately, the redistribution of the national produce is entirely effected through the provisioning of the dead.

When, sometime after 2570 BC, tomb decoration expanded as more wall space became available, new topics were added to the simple provisioning theme: bearers burdened with offerings approaching the tomb, butchers slaughtering oxen, bakers baking bread, and brewers brewing beer. The next thing was to take another step back in time and logic and to show agricultural activities and episodes in the life of herdsmen, fish being caught in large nets, hunters lassoing wild animals, men making papyrus boats, and craftsmen manufacturing items of funerary furniture. Even the Egyptians realized that bread alone was not enough, and pursuits which were not purely materialistic, such as music, dance, and games, also began to be included. All these activities are shown being carried out by minor figures, usually members of the tomb owner's household and people belonging to his estates.

The developed repertory of tomb scenes thus presents a large selection of themes and a number of interesting details, but it was never the result of pure artistic creativity and random inspiration. The freedom of the craftsman or artist responsible for the tomb's decoration was not absolute, but rather consisted of his ability to choose first, the topic (e.g. agriculture, or baking and brewing) and, to a lesser extent, its location in the tomb, then the episodes which were going to be shown (e.g. ploughing, sowing, reaping, threshing, winnowing, and transport), the composition of each episode (e.g. the number of participants and their relationship within the scene), and finally the treatment of individual figures (their gestures, details of clothing, etc.). The artist's originality (and in spite of everything said so far the term is justified since no tombs with identical decoration are known) depended on the choice of a new combination of familiar elements rather than on their invention. The corpus of scenes at the artist's disposal was, of course, enriched from time to time by the inclusion of new subjects or a contemporary treatment of some of the old ones, while others became traditional and after some time ceased to reflect reality. Some topics, however, were never shown because, for various reasons, they never became part of the recognized repertory. This, therefore, means that Egyptian tomb art cannot be taken at its face value, but must be interpreted. To try and reconstruct Egyptian 'daily life' on the basis of tomb representations, as many popular publications are fond of doing, is a risky business. Even greater caution must be exercised when studying representations in Egyptian temples, although scenes in which we could expect to find wild cats occur there very exceptionally.

In which tomb scenes are we then to look for Egyptian wild cats? The period of Egyptian history now conventionally known to Egyptologists as the Old Kingdom (2647–2124 BC) was the era of the great pyramid-builders, whose monuments we admire in the neighbourhood of Memphis (at that time still called Inebhedj), on the west bank of the Nile some 20km to the south-west of present Cairo. The royal pyramids at Giza, Abusir, Saqqara, Dahshur, Meidum and several other places are surrounded by tombs of officials and priests. These tombs are known as *mastaba*s (from the Arabic word for 'bench,' describing the external shape of the tombs' superstructures) and the walls of their free-standing chapels are decorated with scenes in raised relief. Stone was the material in which to build for eternity because of its permanence, and relief-carving was preferred to painting for the same reason. Priests and visitors were allowed access to the chapel; the underground burial chamber was sealed and inaccessible. After *c.*2300 BC, decorated private tombs, mostly rock-cut, became more common in provincial cemeteries also.

Many Old-Kingdom tombs show the deceased standing tall in a small papyrus skiff, hurling a throwstick at birds, spearing fish or, usually in the case of women, pulling or shaking the stalks of papyrus plants. These are exceptional representations because the tomb owner is actively engaged in a demanding physical exercise. In most other instances he remains an attentive but passive observer, standing in a dignified posture, seated, or carried in a palanquin, while others provide the hustle and bustle which is so characteristic of Egyptian tomb reliefs. Such scenes almost certainly did not reflect reality, but had symbolic meaning which went well beyond the outwardly simple record of hunting and fishing. It is difficult to explain them in an entirely satisfactory manner, but one wonders whether they may be connected with a concept which is often taken up as a theme in Egyptian art, that of the necessity to assert control over the forces of nature, here symbolized by the birds and fish. According to the Egyptian ideas concerning kingship this was

15 The ichneumon (*Herpestes ichneumon*) is a vicious raider of birds' nests, but also a courageous snake-fighter.

the duty of the pharaoh, but we may have here one of the earliest instances of 'democratization' of the very ancient prerogatives of the ruler (dating to well before the beginning of the historic period) and their transfer to the other groups of society. Other examples of this process are known. Another possible explanation is that the scene was at first part of the repertory of the royal pyramid temples which was later adopted, with a modified symbolic content, for the decoration of private tombs. Activities in the marshes in which the tomb owner's personnel are involved often accompany the main themes, and include papyrus-gathering and making small papyrus boats, netting fish and fowl, angling, hunting hippopotami, and light-hearted river-battles between boat-crews in which punting poles are used without mercy. Animals, birds, fish, insects, and plants provide a colourful setting.

An occasional inclusion in these scenes of the ichneumon, also known as the mongoose, is of particular interest. Two species have been reported from Egypt in modern times. *Herpestes ichneumon* is an animal with an elongated body, pointed head, characteristically round ears, relatively short legs, and a long tail. Its rather coarse fur is of a grizzled dark colour. It is reminiscent of a large weasel or a rat and only a little smaller than the Egyptian wild cat, with a body-length of some 500–600mm and a tail which is not much shorter. The ichneumon can successfully fight snakes and rats, but is also a vicious raider of birds' nests. In the second half of the first century BC, Diodorus Siculus described it appreciatively as a destroyer of crocodiles' eggs. His account of how it kills crocodiles is considerably less believable. According to him, the ichneumon first rolls in mud (perhaps in order to acquire camouflage for concealment or to form a protective carapace, but the author does not explain this further). When it sees a crocodile asleep with its mouth open, it jumps into it and destroys the beast by gnawing its intestines from inside. Classical authors recount several similarly fantastic stories about Egyptian animals. While modern scholars bravely try to explain them by references to complex religious concepts to which the stories are supposed to allude, one cannot help feeling that they may reflect a sense of humour and mischievous leg-pulling of gullible foreigners by the Egyptians rather than lack of observation of nature or intentional obscurantism.

The ichneumon is shown in a number of tombs at Saqqara which date to the advanced Old Kingdom, *c.*2300–2150 BC. Usually it can be found in a small cameo scene where it is eagerly climbing a papyrus stalk, which bends under its weight, in search of a bird's nest. Reality and artistic licence almost certainly merge here: the conventions of Egyptian art required a base-line on which to place individual figures, and while in most cases these were straight horizontal lines separating registers, the base-line is in these cases provided by a single papyrus stalk. The weight of the animal makes such a

16 An ichneumon grasped by its tail, on a wall relief in the tomb of Mereruka, the vizier of King Teti (2311–2281 BC) at Saqqara.

feat somewhat unlikely in real life. It would be hardly possible to mistake the ichneumon for another animal because of its characteristic silhouette, with the upper outline of the pointed head continuing smoothly and fluently as a gently curved line along the back of its body and the long tail. In the tomb-chapel of the vizier Mereruka at Saqqara, dating to the reign of King Teti (2311–2281 BC), there is a curious detail depicting a man firmly grasping an ichneumon's tail. The relative sizes of the man and animal do not correspond here to our perception of reality; this was one of the more flexible aspects of Egyptian representations, which the artist skilfully exploited in order to link in one scene the large figure of the tomb owner and the ichneumon, shown on a corresponding scale, with the much smaller representations of the minor participants. One wonders whether the planes of the real world and make-believe became one here and whether perhaps a tame animal was meant to distract the attention of wild fowl so that they would present an easier target for Mereruka's throwstick. Instances of tame ichneumons kept in Egyptian houses in order to control vermin are known from relatively recent times.

Another ichneumon is shown descending a papyrus stalk with a chick in its jaws. In a relief in the tomb of Princess Seshseshet Idut, which is also at Saqqara and is of approximately the same date, the dark brown paint on the ichneumon's fur, perhaps with some indication of the individual hairs, is still well preserved. The ichneumon remained a constant element of the fishing and fowling scenes. It can be found in the tomb of Khnumhotep III at Beni Hasan in c.1900 BC and, as a rather cuddly animal with little claim to realism, in the tomb of Menna at Thebes (TT 69), which is some 900 years later than the *mastaba* of Mereruka.

In her tomb, Princess Seshseshet is standing in a papyrus boat smelling a lotus flower, as a concession to her femininity, but otherwise the marsh-scene is designed very much like those showing the more masculine pursuits of

17 A genet and an ichneumon above a scene showing the netting of fish and the harpooning of hippopotami, on a painted wall-relief in the tomb of princess Seshseshet Idut, probably of the reign of King Teti (2311–2281 BC), at Saqqara.

34

18 The genet (*Genetta genetta*) can be confused with the cat (*Felis silvestris libyca* or *Felis chaus*) when interpreting Egyptian representations, although in reality the two animals are quite different.

fishing and fowling. In addition to the ichneumon, another animal is depicted plundering a bird's nest. It has a narrow pointed muzzle, long ears, a very long tail, and a coat of sallow-grey colour. One unfortunate chick is already dangling from its jaws, and the same cruel fate, it seems, is awaiting the other four fledglings in the nest. Their parents are frantically trying to distract the bloodthirsty marauder. The animal is a genet (probably *Genetta genetta*), the smallest of the predators which used to stalk the marshes, but now regarded as extinct in Egypt. Its body-length is around 450mm; the tail measures some 300mm or more. The genet can usually be easily recognized by the characteristic dark lines on the neck which turn into spots on the body, and the dark rings on the tail, but the relief in Seshseshet's tomb has unfortunately lost such subtle colour distinctions. Two genets and one ichneumon can be seen in the same context in the somewhat earlier tomb of the official Ty at Saqqara. Ty held a number of offices connected with pyramids and sun-temples of kings dating between *c.*2450 and 2370 BC and may have been the contemporary of the last of them, King Nyuserra. There is little doubt that in spite of the artist's success in conveying the tension of these dramatic events shown unfolding in the animal world, this was a popular and conventionally stereotyped scene which was regarded as standard for the decoration of these tombs.

The genet's coat markings are very clear on the three animals represented in the tomb of Khnumhotep III at Beni Hasan. Around 2123 BC power in Egypt was seized by rulers who hailed from Henen-nesu (classical Heracleo-polis, modern Ihnasya el-Medina in Middle Egypt), while contenders appeared in the south, in Weset (Thebes, modern Luxor). The reasons for this development were complex, partly inherent in the system itself and its

19 A scene of fish-spearing in the tomb of Khnumhotep III at Beni Hasan, *c.*1900 BC. The tall rushes conceal a cat, two genets and an ichneumon.

20 The cat in the marshes, a wall-painting in the tomb of Khnumhotep III at Beni Hasan, *c*.1900 BC, recorded by Howard Carter.

inability to reform, partly climatic (a series of low Niles). The old institutions of the state, including workshops with craftsmen and artists who built and decorated tombs and maintained the artistic tradition, either collapsed or were forced to operate in different, much more modest, conditions. Because the central authority was weakened, local rulers, particularly those in Middle Egypt (Asyut, Beni Hasan), gained an unprecedented degree of autonomy which, as always in Egypt, was faithfully reflected in the increased size and improved quality of decoration of their tombs. Eventually, around 2040 BC, Egypt was once again united by the Theban kings who ushered in the period usually known as the Middle Kingdom (2040–1648 BC), but the most powerful of the local administrators were able to retain some of their privileges for a while longer. Khnumhotep III was such a district administrator at Beni Hasan during the reigns of Amenemhat II and Senusret II, around *c*.1900 BC. His tomb is a real treasury of representations of animals, albeit rather naively portrayed. The painted decoration in the main room of his tomb-chapel includes marsh-scenes which unmistakably imitate their Old-Kingdom proto-types, but are also considerably different because of the changed historical, religious and artistic circumstances. A genet is shown scrambling among the rushes in the fowling scene, and another two are present in Khnumhotep's fishing scene.

We must, however, return briefly to Old-Kingdom tombs in order to clarify a probable misunderstanding which is responsible for the alleged earliest reference to the cat, presumably wild, in Egyptian tomb-scenes. This is in the *mastaba* of Meryre-nufer, also called Qar, a high official who was in charge of the settlements of priests and craftsmen attached to the pyramids of Khufu (2549–2526 BC) and Menkaura (2488–2460 BC) and probably lived during the reign of Pepy I (2280–2243 BC). It is situated in the eastern part of the necropolis at Giza. When it was excavated by G. A. Reisner, A. Rowe and T. R. D. Greenless in 1924–5, two small relief fragments were found and in the relatively recent publication of the tomb by Wm. K. Simpson they were assigned to the decoration of the staircase connecting the superstructure of the tomb with the rock-cut underground chapel. It seems that one of the fragments shows an ichneumon, while the animal on the other was described as a 'cat climbing . . . [a] stalk to [a] duck nest.' The 'cat' is shown carrying a bird by the neck in its mouth. Unfortunately, the reliefs were only recorded in sketches in the object register of the excavation and were not photo-graphed. Nowadays it is no longer possible to locate the fragments in order to check them because they have probably disappeared into one of the many closely-guarded storerooms of the Egyptian Antiquities Organization. The sketch does, indeed, appear to show a cat, with pointed ears, a short muzzle, and long legs, but caution demands that this relief be treated with scepticism. It would have been easy to mistake the silhouette of a genet for that of a cat when making a sketch under difficult field conditions. Furthermore, the archaeologist who recorded the monument may have known and subcon-sciously imitated a more completely preserved relief in the Museo Gregoriano in the Vatican. This displays a similar composition: two genets and, this time unmistakably, a cat are climbing papyrus stalks towards birds' nests. For a long time this relief used to be dated to about 2400 or 2300 BC, and only relatively recently has it been established that it is some 1700 years later and comes from the Theban tomb (TT 34) of the 'fourth prophet of the god Amun,' Montuemhat, dated to the mid-seventh century BC. The continuity of motifs in Egyptian art can sometimes be a source of some difficulties.

The tomb of Khnumhotep III (*c*.1900 BC) at Beni Hasan, has already been mentioned several times. A large scene next to the entrance to the shrine with a statue, shows the tomb owner spearing fish in the traditional way.

While the subject matter is well-known, the artist adopted several interesting solutions to the problems of space and perspective (the Egyptian concept of the latter, sometimes called 'aspective,' was rather different from that prevalent in modern Western art). Thus the water with the fish about to be impaled on Khnumhotep's harpoon rises vertically like a mound, with the papyrus thicket forming its background. The animals are no longer shown in a semi-realistic fashion climbing a single papyrus stalk but are placed directly among the papyrus plants, as if the artist experimented with the amalgamation of the horizontal and vertical planes into one. Beside the traditional ichneumon and genets the artist introduced a new feature: the cat. The animal is only a minor element of the scene's setting and appears to have no religious or overtly symbolic significance. It sits on its haunches on one of the stalks which bends under its weight and so provides an almost straight horizontal

21 Two genets and a cat searching for birds' nests in the marsh, on a relief from the Theban tomb-chapel of Montuemhat, c.650 BC. Vatican, Museo Gregoriano Egizio.

22 Animals from the desert margins, in a hunting scene in the tomb of Khnumhotep III at Beni Hasan, *c*.1900 BC. It is doubtful that the seated cat is *Felis silvestris libyca*.

base-line for the representation. The cat's tail, partly obscured by the right haunch on the inside of which it curls, points straight up, the standard 'hiero-glyphic' image of the animal. The cat was accurately recorded in watercolours by Howard Carter in his pre-Tutankhamun days (his paintings of animals and birds are famous): the body is grey-brown without any markings, but with four or more dark rings on the tail and three darker bands on the front paws. The forehead, throat and underbelly of the animal are almost white. The whiskers are long.

There are two questions to be answered: which species of the Egyptian cat is shown here, and whether the animal is wild or domesticated. Commenting on Carter's drawing nearly a hundred years ago, the brilliant British Egyptol-ogist Francis Llewellyn Griffith suggested that this was *Felis maniculata* (i.e. *Felis silvestris libyca*) because of its long and tapering tail. Quoting no lesser authority than J. Anderson, the author of several fundamental books on Egyp-tian fauna, he claimed that this was a domesticated cat. Griffith's approach to the representation was rather too literal and both views require revision. The cat is shown in its 'hieroglyphic' image which, as we shall see later, had by then been well established. It seems that just as the Egyptians did not distinguish lexicographically between different wild cats (and also the domesticated cat), they adopted only one 'cat' image which, with minor variants (particularly the position of the cat's tail), was used as a 'hieroglyph' in their writing. It was this iconography of the cat which the artist used here, but the complete absence of body markings (in total contrast to the two genets in the same scene) and the marshy setting indicate that the cat represented is *Felis chaus*. The long tail of the cat, which is more appropriate for *Felis silvestris libyca*, is probably due to the standardized hieroglyphic prototype. There is little to support the view that this is a domesticated cat because of the absence of any sign of a direct relationship with the tomb owner. Griffith was aware of this difficulty and pointed out that the domestic cat tends to stray and hunt for itself; while this is certainly true, it is hardly a compelling argument when interpreting this scene. It is, then, most likely that this is a wild cat, and probably *Felis chaus*.

The theme of the hunting of fowl and the spearing of fish in the marshes continued to be very common in the tombs of the Theban nobles and priests, mostly dating between *c*.1500 and 1350 BC. The latter part of the Middle Kingdom, after 1800 BC, saw progressive weakening of the central authority which culminated in a takeover by a group of immigrants from Western Asia, the Hyksos (an Egyptian term for their leaders, literally 'rulers of foreign countries'), around 1648 BC. Once again, it was the local princes in the south, at Weset (Thebes), who offered the strongest opposition to the Hyksos rule and eventually succeeded in wresting power from their hands. The new period of strongly centralized government which followed is called the New Kingdom (1540–1069 BC) by Egyptologists. Theban topography favoured rock-cut tombs, and the pharaohs started being buried in the Valley of the Kings, while private tombs were made over a large area of the Theban west bank. The details of New-Kingdom fowling and fishing scenes betray how far they came to be removed from reality: for a trip to the marshes and strenuous exercise the tomb owner is dressed in fine clothes, wears jewellery and is accompanied by his whole family. We shall have an opportunity to return to several of these scenes later but one of them, of Menna (TT 69), dating to the reigns of Thutmose IV and Amenhotep III (*c*.1390 BC), is of particular interest. There is the ubiquitous ichneumon climbing a papyrus stalk, but the other animal is a cat, with a yellow-brown striped coat and a long tail, certainly *Felis silvestris libyca*. Is this a variation on the wild animals which we have already seen in the tomb of Khnumhotep III at Beni Hasan? Or is it a domesticated cat taking part in an imaginary family outing? This question, unfortunately, cannot be answered with absolute certainty, but I believe that this is a domestic cat. As we shall see, there is little doubt that by this time the animal had been domesticated, and since the composition is fictitious and does not reflect reality, the inclusion of a domestic cat is not a contradiction but a logical extension of the theme.

Few of the activities shown in Egyptian tombs take place on desert margins. The hunting of wild game is a conspicuous exception although it remained only infrequently shown during the Old Kingdom (2647–2124 BC). Disappointingly, none of these scenes shows a wild cat in which we would recognize *Felis silvestris libyca* or *Felis chaus*.

It has been suggested that a wild cat is represented among the animals in the hunting scene, though apparently not hunted itself, painted in the Theban tomb of the vizier Intefiqer (TT 60), of the reign of Senusret I (1960–1916 BC), but the identification is far from certain. Once again, the remarkable artist who decorated the tomb of Khnumhotep III at Beni Hasan around

23 There may be an intentional humorous touch present in this wall-painting in the Theban tomb of Menna, *c.*1390 BC, as a tabby cat gets first to the eggs in the marsh scene while a rather ponderous-looking ichneumon lags behind.

24 Neferhotep, *c.*1450 BC, was an enthusiastic but hardly discerning hunter. Some would see a cat (*Felis silvestris libyca*) in the animal in the top right corner.

*c.*1900 BC blazed the trail. On the north wall of Khnumhotep's tomb-chapel there is a large display of scenes which include several registers of hunting scenes. The hunt is presented as a sporting occasion: the tomb owner and his sons, accompanied by their hounds, are shown sending a cloud of arrows among a variety of animals. Not all of them are necessarily hunted; some just provide an attractive backdrop for the scene and illustrate the variety and richness of wildlife. Most of them are real, such as the lion, caracal, gazelle, ibex, hare, hedgehog, and zoril, but there is also a curious mythical beast which appears to sprout a head and wings on its back. These seem to have been very much in vogue among the artists decorating the tombs at Beni Hasan. As we shall see, similar creatures were represented on the so-called magic knives of approximately the same period and regarded as benign apotropaic (protective) animals. It is curious how easily reality and fantasy mixed, or perhaps just were not distinguishable. Among these animals there is a seated cat, although to which species it belongs is by no means certain. Its fur is reddish brown but, apparently, without any markings, and its rather thick long tail points up away from the body. It could be *Felis silvestris libyca* or, like the animal standing behind it, a caracal (*Caracal caracal*). It is a great pity that the tombs at Beni Hasan have not been re-recorded in more recent times and that we have to rely on P. E. Newberry's publication which, while pioneering at the end of the last century, is no longer satisfactory.

In the Theban tomb of Neferhotep (TT A.5), of the reign of Thutmose III (1479–1425 BC) or Amenhotep II (1427–1401 BC), there is an animal shown as having been hit with one of the tomb owner's arrows. It has been suggested that it is *Felis chaus* because of its short tail and tufted ears. This detail is only known from a copy by F. Cailliaud published in 1823. The tomb has either been destroyed or is lost, and the identification of the animal is not safe. It would be the only known instance of an indigenous small wild cat being hunted.

To sum up, our search for representations of wild cats in ancient Egypt has produced rather meagre results. Apparently the wild cats were not shown in the reliefs and paintings in Egyptian tombs and temples during the third millennium BC. The reasons for this may have been that the ichneumon and the genet were a more common sight in the papyrus thickets along the Nile banks at that time and that the tightly controlled repertory did not provide sufficient opportunities for the inclusion of cats. Desert scenes occurred too infrequently in Old-Kingdom tombs. Early in the second millennium BC the situation changed only a little. The painted scenes in the tomb of Khnumhotep III at Beni Hasan, dated to *c.*1900 BC, may show both indigenous small wild cats, *Felis chaus* as well as *Felis silvestris libyca*. The cats in the similar scenes in later tombs, such as those of Menna (TT 69, *c.*1390 BC) and Montuemhat (TT 34, *c.*650 BC), both apparently *Felis silvestris libyca*, are almost certainly already domesticated. The scanty attention paid to the wild cats does not prepare us for the change which took place once they decided to throw in their lot with humanity. But that is the next chapter of the story.

Together at last
The domestic cats

Considering the initial usefulness, then the popularity, and finally the religious importance of the cat, it would be most satisfying to be able to state firmly and unambiguously that the domestication of the animal took place in Egypt, to trace and illustrate the successive stages of this development, and to assign them accurate dates. The history of the Egyptian cat is better known than those of its relatives anywhere else in the world, but such certainty, unfortunately, eludes us on all counts.

Remains of cats found at Near Eastern sites such as Jericho (late sixth or early fifth millennium BC, and perhaps already c.9000 BC) are earlier than the corresponding finds from Egypt but their scarcity in both regions suggests that the chances of preservation play an inordinately influential role in domestication theories. The evidence provided by skeletal material of the predynastic period (before c.3000 BC) from Egypt is encouraging but not more than that. The earliest known remains of a cat in Egypt come from Mostagedda, south of Asyut in Middle Egypt, and are dated to sometime before c.4000 BC. One of the graves in this cemetery contained the burial of a man who, judging by the tools and other material accompanying him to the next world, probably was a primitive craftsman. The bones of a gazelle and a cat, the former probably intended for his funerary repast, the latter perhaps his pet, were found at the dead man's feet. The excavation of the late predynastic settlement at Abydos in Upper Egypt yielded skeletal evidence for the cat dating to just before 3000 BC, but it is not possible to establish whether it was wild, tame or domesticated. Such uncertainty also plagues material of somewhat later dates, e.g. from Elephantine, near Aswan, dated between c.2500 and 1900 BC. More often than not, an animal that had become a pet would have been buried regardless of whether it had started life wild or domesticated, and conclusions based on isolated instances of such discoveries are unsafe. The finds of mummified cats do not predate the first millennium BC. There is little doubt that by then the animal had been fully domesticated and the difficulties which accompany attempts at distinguishing between these and wild cats have already been mentioned.

Textual evidence concerning cats before the beginning of the New Kingdom (1540 BC) is very restricted. It is perhaps appropriate that the oldest certain images of cats in ancient Egypt occur as hieroglyphs. The earliest

25   The three 'hieroglyphic cats' on a fragment of a wall-relief found at Lisht, but possibly from the cult-temple of Pepy II (2236–2143 BC) at Saqqara. New York, MMA.

appear on a small fragment of a temple wall found in the vicinity of the pyramid of King Amenemhat I (1980–1951 BC) at el-Lisht, on the west bank of the Nile some 50km south of Cairo. Amenemhat I was the successor of the Theban rulers who, after a period of internal strife, united the country under their control around 2040 BC and inaugurated a new period of strong centralized government, the Middle Kingdom (2040–1648 BC). The king probably came to the throne as the result of a *coup d'état*, but that did not adversely affect his successful reign during which Egypt flourished. The need to replace Thebes as the royal residence soon became apparent and a new state capital was established near modern Lisht. It became known as Itjtawy, literally 'Seizer of the Two Lands,' from its full name 'Amenemhat I is the Seizer of the Two Lands (= both parts of Egypt).' Artificially-created towns and villages were often given such long-winded names. Thebes, because of its location deep in the south, was not ideally suited to be the administrative centre of the whole of Egypt and there must have been reasons, most probably connected with the movement and silting up of the branches of the Nile, which made it difficult to return to the former Old-Kingdom capital further north, just south of Cairo.

The pyramid of Amenemhat I was now constructed in the vicinity of the new royal residence, and in order to save building costs, and perhaps for other reasons, his architects exploited the dilapidated structures of the earlier kings at Giza and Saqqara as convenient sources of material. One limestone block from such a building seems to date to the end of the Old Kingdom, perhaps to the reign of Pepy II (2236–2143 BC), although the dating is based only on stylistic criteria (thus the possibility remains that the relief may be later, c.1950 BC). It is part of a scene showing an anonymous male deity described as 'lord of the city of Miuu.' The name of the town is written with three hieroglyphs representing seated cats, all facing left. It may be that the name of the locality was, indeed, 'Cats' (the hieroglyphic sign repeated three times conveyed multitude and so recorded grammatical plural) or 'Cat Town,' although it was in the nature of the Egyptian script that the name need not have anything to do with cats and their images may have only been used to record its pronunciation. The hieroglyph appears in two variants: two of the cats are shown with their tail gently curling away from and above the body, parallel to the line of the animal's back, while that of the third animal curls up along its left haunch at its side. This last was later to become the standard 'hieroglyphic' image of the cat. It is unfortunate that the name of the god is lost and that the town is not known from elsewhere. A Ptolemaic (after 332 BC) locality near Medinet Habu in the Theban area which had a similar name is known from demotic papyri, and would have been connected with a genuine cattery in a local temple precinct.

The Egyptians were quite fond of naming their children after animals, probably because something in their character or behaviour reminded them of a similar characteristic observed in the animal world. There are many examples, from 'Frog,' 'Mouse,' 'Gazelle' and 'Monkey' to 'Wolf,' 'Hound,' 'Crocodile' and 'Hippopotamus.' Most people, it seems, had only one name although instances of two names are not uncommon. Very long and often rather pompous names were shortened and nicknames were frequent; many of the theriophoric (after animals) names probably belong to the latter category. 'Cat' could be applied to men (*Pa-miu*, 'The Tomcat') as well as women (*Miut* or *Miit*, later with the definite article, *Ta-miit*, 'The Cat'), but female names are known from considerably earlier.

Personal names which might derive from this word are known from the late Old Kingdom. One of the daughters of Iymery at Giza, around 2400 BC, was called *Mit*, but the name is written phonetically, without a hieroglyph which would confirm that the intended meaning was 'cat,' and since other possibilities exist, perhaps we should not put too much trust in this interpretation. *Miut*, the name of a servant woman shown sieving flour on the stela (gravestone) of a certain Tefnen from Giza, dated to c.2311–2140 BC, is followed by a hieroglyph of a lying or crouching cat. Its very long tail seems to curl along its haunch and then stretch in a wavy fashion behind and away

26 Two daughters of a man called Mentuhotep, buried at Saqqara *c.*1950 BC, were called *Miit*, 'Female Cat' (near the bottom of the broken stela).

from the animal. The next female 'Cat' (*Miit*) was a five-year old girl who belonged to the household of King Mentuhotep II (2050–1999 BC). She must have died unexpectedly: her mummy was found in the king's temple at Deir el-Bahri, on the west bank of the Nile at Thebes, buried in coffins which were much too big for her and on which the name of the original owner had been rather crudely changed to hers. The name is written with hieroglyphs conveying the phonetic spelling followed by a sign showing a seated cat, with its tail curling up along its back. In another contemporary name, that of the mother of Intef (a high official serving the same king), the hieroglyph of a cat shows an animal whose tail points almost straight up. Two daughters of a man called Mentuhotep, who lived around 1950 BC and whose stela was found at Saqqara, were also called *Miit*. The names are written with a sign showing a 'hicroglyphic' cat with its tail curling along its haunch.

Our main source of information on the domestication of the cat is art. Physical appearance is not a very good indicator of whether an animal is domesticated, so we have to rely on the context in which it occurs and on the frequency of its representations on the walls of tombs. We have, however, already seen in the example of the wild cats that the link between reality and Egyptian art is not simple and that the presence or absence of a motif must not be interpreted uncritically.

The cat in a domestic context appears for the first time at Beni Hasan in Middle Egypt, in the tomb of Baket III. This official called himself 'Great Overlord of the Oryx-district (= Beni Hasan) in its Entirety,' i.e. he was a local administrator in charge of one of some forty districts among which

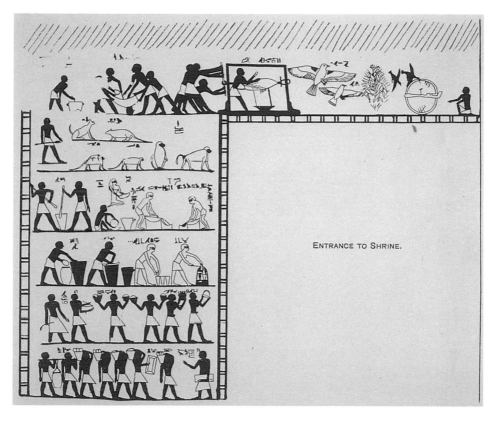

ENTRANCE TO SHRINE.

27 A confrontation between a cat and a rat in a painted scene in the tomb of Baket III at Beni Hasan, *c.*1950 BC.

Egypt was divided. Baket probably lived around *c.*1950 BC. In his rock-cut chapel, on the wall next to the entrance to a small shrine which housed his statue, are various painted representations. Above the door there are men engaged in activities connected with the vintage, including the pressing of the must in a sack, and the trapping of birds in a large clap-net. Below, to the left of the entrance, are five registers of scenes. The lower four show rather standard depictions of bakers, brewers and offering-bearers. The top register is the most interesting by far and contains several animals, each with a 'caption' which identifies it: a female cat (*mit*) confronting a field rat (probably *Arvicanthis niloticus*), and four adult baboons, one of them with a baby baboon on her back. Descriptive captions, comparable to those in our cartoons, were traditional in Egyptian two-dimensional representations and should not be interpreted as a sign of lack of confidence of the artist in the quality of his work. In Old-Kingdom tombs (2647–2124 BC) they played an important role by neatly filling the empty area between representations (to leave a space would have been regarded as artistically uncouth). They also extended the information provided by the images (e.g. by recording the conversation between the represented people) but here they degenerated into mere identifiers. The cat, facing right, is shown in its 'hieroglyphic' form, with the tail gently curling up and partly obscured by the right haunch. A man stands at the left end of the register, holding a stick reminiscent of the instrument often seen in the hands of house attendants looking after pet animals. This was a baton with one of its ends shaped like a human hand. There is no way of knowing whether the cat is domesticated or just tamed, but there is little doubt that the animal is an accepted member of the household and not just a passing visitor. The inclusion of the rat must be significant and indicates the cat's usefulness and value as a pest-destroyer.

Another monument, a fragment of a tomb wall of approximately the same

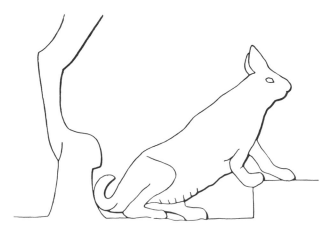

28 A dog or a cat? The controversy continues. A relief-decorated wall-fragment from Koptos, *c.*1950 BC. London, Petrie Museum.

date, is more ambiguous. It is a stone slab which the famous British archaeologist Flinders Petrie found re-used in the pavement of the severely damaged temple of the god Min at Koptos (modern Qift in Upper Egypt). On one side of the stone we see the legs of a man, facing left. He is seated on a chair under which is his dog, rather poetically named as Hemuma, 'Steering-Oar of the Lion,' perhaps because of his tail. Representations of dogs are often accompanied by their names, which sometimes refer to their appearance: 'Ebony,' 'Black,' 'Big.' Although the dog is shown under the man's chair, this need not be taken too literally. The animal may be sitting next to it and in any case, as we have seen, leaving large unused spaces went against the Egyptian understanding of good composition, so the representation of the animal was used as a convenient space-filler.

On the reverse of the Koptos block there is a similar scene, only this time the man is accompanied by his wife and both are facing right. The woman is seated close to her husband on the same wide chair but, according to the rules of Egyptian 'perspective', she is shown as if she were well behind him and further away from the viewer, i.e. partly obscured by the man and to his left. Under her chair, there is an animal in which the excavator initially saw the form of a dog. It is a plump, ungainly creature with short pointed ears, a short blunt face, and a short curled-up tail. The Egyptologist A.J. Arkell subsequently suggested that the animal is a cat. The representation is far removed from the sleek elegance of a real cat and Arkell's theory has not been accepted by everybody. Current opinion has swung back to the original identification by Petrie. It must be admitted that several of the animal's characteristics are puzzling, and the short curling tail is particularly difficult to explain. Nevertheless, two additional considerations may be adduced.

First, the animal has no name, and cats, unlike dogs, were not given names. The only exception seems to be the cat in the tomb of Puimre at Thebes (TT 39), dated to the reign of Thutmose III (1479–1425 BC), which is called *Nedjem* (or *Nedjemet*, if female), 'Sweet' or 'Pleasant;' the figure of the cat is, unfortunately, almost completely lost.

Second, the animal is shown next to the seated woman (the pairing of men with dogs, and women with cats, later became a regular feature).

So it may be that this is one of the instances – which must have existed but usually pass unmentioned in books – of a less than competent artist, in this case trying to portray a tame or domesticated cat. The posture of the cat, with its front paws on a raised platform on which the man and his wife rest their feet, is unusual but not unique. The cat under the chair of a seated lady became a standard convention in Egyptian art some 500 years later.

So far, we have noted only isolated representations of cats accompanying people around 1950 BC but, as we shall see, this corresponded to the appearance of the cat as one of the 'protective animals' in religious beliefs. The word 'cat' began to be used as a personal name a few hundred years earlier. Small amulets representing cats may also date to between *c*.2300 and 2040 BC. Other indications of increased intimacy between cats and people can be found and cited as evidence for a change in their mutual relationship.

At Abydos, the most important Middle-Kingdom cemetery in Upper Egypt, Flinders Petrie found a small tomb with a pyramidal superstructure which he dated to *c*.1980–1801 BC. In its chapel, there were seventeen skeletons of cats and nearby a row of small offering pots which the excavator estimated may have originally contained milk. This would be the earliest recorded instance of adult cats being given milk which, as wild animals, they would not taste after they had been weaned. Diodorus mentions that the Egyptians used to feed cats with bread in milk, or with raw cut-up fish, and that they called them with a special clucking sound.

An alabaster vessel in the shape of a cat, of about the same date, is the earliest large three-dimensional representation of a cat. The animal's eyes are inlaid with rock crystal over a painted pupil and lined with copper. The

29 An alabaster vessel, perhaps intended to hold cosmetic oil, in the form of a cat, *c*.1980–1801 BC. This is the earliest three-dimensional representation of a cat on a larger scale. New York, MMA.

30 An early faience statuette of a cat, possibly from Sheikh Abd el-Qurna (Thebes), *c.*1850–1650 BC. British Museum.

incised lines on the body probably imitate the tabby marking of the animal's coat. The vessel has remarkably thin walls and would have been used as a container for cosmetic oil or similar material.

A blue faience statuette of a stalking cat with a spotted coat, from Matariya (Heliopolis), is similarly dated, as is the faience statuette of a lying, perhaps sleeping, cat found in a tomb near the pyramid of Senusret I (1960–1916 BC) at Lisht. A cat with its back arched, as if about to jump, and with the markings of its fur indicated by dark dashes, comes, together with another, crouching, cat from a tomb of *c.*1850–1650 BC at Abydos. Another small sculpture which belongs to this group comes, allegedly, from Thebes. These cats are so realistically portrayed that one is reluctant to assign them a function similar to that of the vicious cats represented on magic knives. But this may be a sentimental notion which has no place here.

Each of the gold spacer-bars from a bracelet of Sobekemsaf, the queen of the Theban King Intef v (1648–1643 BC), is decorated with three reclining cats with their front paws crossed.

From about 1450 BC, cats in a domestic context became frequent in Theban tombs and they began to be shown so obviously at ease in Egyptian houses that there can be little doubt that these had been domesticated animals for some time. There is no compelling evidence to suggest that the domesticated cat was introduced to Egypt from abroad, and the country provided all the

31 Gold spacer-bars of Sobekemsaf, the queen of Intef v (1648–1643 BC), with three reclining cats. Possibly from Edfu. British Museum.

necessary preconditions for the domestication process to take place there. We can only speculate about how this happened and try to reconstruct a sequence of the events from the available pieces of this jigsaw puzzle.

The living conditions in Egyptian towns, villages and country estates varied as much as the social status of their inhabitants, from the cramped squalor of urban housing through primitive peasant dwellings to spacious and comfortable country villas. Animals were never far away and those which were domesticated played a vital part in the country's economy. There were herds of cattle, sheep, goats and donkeys. Pigs were reared, although they were almost never shown in tomb scenes. A large variety of geese, duck and cranes were bred in fowlyards. Hunting dogs are attested in Egypt very early, after *c.*4000 BC, and they are shown in this capacity, and also as household pets, in tombs. Baboons and monkeys were also bred in captivity because in Egypt they no longer lived in the wild and had to be imported from the south. The horse was introduced from Western Asia, probably early during the Hyksos domination in the seventeenth century BC, but its use as a draught animal remained confined to two-wheeled chariots. There were no horse-drawn waggons, mainly because the Nile was such a convenient traffic artery that roads were not required. Very heavy items, such as building blocks or large statues, had to be moved only short distances overland, and here the cattle-drawn sled or human force were the traditional means of transport. The horse was occasionally ridden but never replaced the donkey in this role. In the absence of the camel, the donkey was also the only pack animal suited for long caravan journeys across the desert.

Two potential dangers threatened the life and prosperity of the Egyptians of any social status indoors as well as outdoors: poisonous snakes, and voracious rats and mice. The cobras (*Naja haje* and *Naja nigricollis*) and vipers (*Cerastes cerastes*, or horned viper, and *Cerastes vipera*) were encountered much too often for comfort and their bite was deadly. Rats and mice attacked supplies of grain in estate granaries and communal silos in towns. There was little that men could do personally to safeguard against these hazards and so it is easy to see why animals able to destroy such vermin were not only tolerated but made welcome. The wild cat (*Felis silvestris libyca*) would have strayed into settlements and recognized granaries and silos as ready-made killing grounds. There would also have been occasional scraps of food either discarded or left on purpose to encourage the cats to return. Eventually a kind of symbiosis was reached which suited both sides: in exchange for a steady supply of food, or access to it, cats kept the area clean of vermin.

The relationship reminds me strongly of another which I have been able to observe in modern Egypt on many occasions. Sites with ancient Egyptian remains are looked after by the Egyptian Antiquities Organization whose local inspectors assign guards, *ghaffirs*, to protect individual monuments. These guards stay on site at all times, often alone, and live in small huts put up for that purpose. This may be a fairly pleasant and profitable occupation if the place is visited by tourists who, as a reward for small courtesies and some informal guiding, provide a much-needed supplement to the *ghaffirs'* very modest wages. Unfortunately, many of the monuments are in areas where the *ghaffir* does not see a living soul for days on end and his stay there is one of unrelieved boredom. Vigilance is needed, however, not only because of the possibility of an unexpected visit by his superiors but also because of the real danger to the monument in his care posed by looters and robbers. The *ghaffirs* therefore usually strike up a kind of symbiotic relationship with the many feral dogs who roam the desert margins and the outskirts of villages and towns in large packs. The always-hungry dogs are fed leftovers so that they adopt the area around the *ghaffir's* dwelling as their home ground. The *ghaffir* can then spend most of the day in his hut, safe in the knowledge that the approach of any visitor will be announced well in advance by the dogs barking furiously as they try to deter the interloper. The dogs go with the territory; they do not belong to anybody and at the end of his tour of duty, usually several weeks long, the *ghaffir* will depart to another, perhaps more lucrative destination. His successor will, of course, immediately set about establishing his own relationship with the pack.

When cats and people became used to each other's presence and recognized the mutual benefits of their co-existence, the next step towards proper domestication was not too difficult to make. Cats are remarkably well suited for taking advantage of changed living conditions. If I had to venture a guess I would suggest that the natural habitat of their Egyptian wild ancestors was so varied that special alertness to, and ability to exploit, any opportunities as they presented themselves were essential for their survival. It seems quite likely that cats soon extended their activities from the neighbourhood of the granaries and silos closer to houses. There their ability to kill rats, mice and, probably even more importantly, snakes also stood them in good stead. Cats were also able to offer new and different characteristics from the traditional pets such as dogs, baboons and monkeys, and they soon won over the hearts of the Egyptians and came to be accepted in their houses. For cats, the household represented an additional source of food and comfort and, in return, they surrendered some degree of their independence. This allowed humans to influence their genetic make-up, mainly by modifying their diet and by selective breeding. In this way, the cat eventually became a domesticated animal, or to put it more precisely, domesticated itself.

Another interesting but quite different theory concerning the domestication of the cat regards religious motivation as its main reason. In ancient

Egypt, practical and ideological considerations are usually so closely inter-
twined that to try to disentangle them and assign them strict priorities is
often extremely difficult and, indeed, methodologically incorrect. It would
be wrong to dismiss the idea out of hand but at present it is difficult to
reconcile what we know about the modest religious significance of the cat in
the early stages of its domestication with its important role as an economic,
protective and companion animal at the same time.

The usefulness of the Egyptian cat for humans was of a different type than
was the case with the other domesticated animals, and the relationship was
governed by different rules. The crudest form of a 'relationship' between
humans and animals in ancient Egypt was one where the latter represented
a convenient source of food, skin or wool: cattle, pigs, sheep, and fowl. Other
animals were domesticated because they possessed certain characteristics
which made them in some respects superior to men and for which they could
be exploited: the horse's strength, the donkey's ability to carry burdens, the
dog's speed and sense of smell. Yet others, pets such as monkeys and baboons,
were kept for companionship and amusement, and their liberty to opt out of
this one-sided relationship was, accordingly, curtailed. The qualities for
which the cat was appreciated required it to have considerable freedom to
come and go as it pleased and to be, to some extent, a free agent. We are
still able to observe the remnants of these characteristics in our domestic
cats, such as their great ability to adapt to and exploit their surroundings, and
their self-contained independence. Sedentary farming was the fundamental
precondition for the cat's domestication; the cat is basically a farmer's animal,
while the dog is the animal of the roving hunter. This helps to understand
why the domesticated cat appeared in Egypt relatively late and why the corresponding evidence for the dog is so much greater. The dog had been in
contact with man for several thousand years before the cat, and certainly well
before the appearance of permanent farming settlements.

The domestication process in ancient Egypt may have unfolded along the
following chronological lines:

*c.*4000 BC
The first permanent settlements, with their granaries and silos, appear and provide
the basic precondition for the meeting of cats (*Felis silvestris libyca*) and humans;

*c.*4000–2000 BC
Cats and humans establish contact and develop a symbiotic relationship based on
mutual advantages; this gradually leads towards domestication (it appears that the
swamp cat, *Felis chaus*, plays a very little part, if any, in this process);

*c.*2000–1000 BC
The fully domesticated cat is a permanent member of the Egyptian household as an
economic and companion animal;

32 A wall-painting in the Deir el-Medina tomb of Ipuy, with a kitten on Ipuy's lap and the mother-cat under the chair of his wife Duammeres, c.1250 BC.

c.1000 BC–AD 350
Because they are now regarded as manifestations of certain deities, in particular the goddess Bastet, cats are also bred in large numbers in temple catteries.

From the reign of Thutmose III (1479–1425 BC) the cat began to be shown quite frequently in the decoration of Theban tombs. The earliest decorated tombs on the west bank of the Nile at Thebes (opposite modern Luxor) go back to the end of the Old Kingdom (c.2300 BC), but the most spectacular date to between c.1540–1186 BC. The tombs were rock-cut, and the plans of their decorated chapels were variants of a cruciform design (a forecourt, and then a short entrance corridor leading to a very wide but short hall preceding a narrow and deep offering room). The burial chambers were at the bottom of deep shafts starting in the chapels.

The scenes in which cats appear can be divided into four types (one of these, illustrations of the so-called *Book of the Dead*, will be described in the following chapter). The first occurs only in the tomb of the sculptor Ipuy (TT 217), of the reign of Ramses II (1279–1213 BC), in the area of the Theban necropolis known as Deir el-Medina. The men buried in these tombs were craftsmen and artists employed on the decoration of the royal tombs in the Valley of the Kings. Their own tombs display superb technical skills combined with a rather naive freshness of design, sometimes bordering on the unorthodox in detail. This accounts for the uniqueness of Ipuy's decoration. The tomb owner and his wife Duammeres, dressed up in their festive clothes, are shown seated on high-backed chairs, while their son and daughter are offering them decorative bouquets. The scene is heavy with symbolism (the word for such a bouquet was *ankh*, from the same root as the word for 'life'), but the artist added a delightful detail in the form of a small kitten on Ipuy's lap. The coat of the kitten is light brown with the tabby pattern indicated by darker stipples. One of its front paws is raised, perhaps a humorous touch since it looks as though it is going to wreck Ipuy's very fine garment. It is, however, possible that this was a posture with which the artist was familiar because it also occurs on the so-called magic knives dated some 500 years earlier and in the contemporary illustrations accompanying the texts of the *Book of the Dead*. In both these cases the cat brandishes a knife, with which it is about to destroy a snake.

An adult cat, with the same coat-colour and markings as the kitten, is seated under the chair of Ipuy's wife. It is possible that it has a collar round its neck (unless the artist tried to indicate the tabby stripes which would have encircled its throat like necklaces). If the animal looks a little strange, this is because its body is represented in the standard 'hieroglyphic' image of a cat,

33 A 'cat under the chair,' wearing a multi-strand bead necklace and heavy earrings, on a wall-painting in the tomb of Penbuy and Kasa at Deir el-Medina, *c.*1250 BC.

but its face is in front view, as if returning a watchful gaze. This was unusual in Egyptian art where the faces, be they of people or animals, were almost always rendered in profile. The cat showing its face can be seen in several other Ramesside tombs, e.g. those of Penbuy and Kasa (TT 10) and Djehutihirmaktuf (TT 357), and it may be that the same local artist drew all these scenes. An earlier example, in a different context, can be found in the tomb of Amenemhat Surero (TT 48), of the reign of Amenhotep III (1391–1353 BC), and also in the tomb of Neferhotep (TT 50), of the reign of Horemheb (1323–1295 BC), and these may have served as the prototypes of the image.

The cat in the tomb of Penbuy and Kasa is a plump and rather cross-looking creature, and one suspects that much of its diet was due to its owners' kindness rather than its own hunting efforts. There is a necklace consisting of three strands of beads round its neck, and it wears earrings with large pendants. This cat would be very much at home in many city flats of today.

This brings us to the second and largest group of nearly twenty scenes with a cat which are known from Theban tombs. These show the tomb owner and his wife seated side by side, sometimes with their children bringing offerings or a priest presenting libation and incense. The cat is invariably under the chair of the wife, perhaps because the animal was more often befriended by the mistress of the house than by her husband. Artistic considerations were also important: the dog had been represented under the chair of the man for some 1000 years before the appearance of the cat and now at last the woman had her companion animal.

Some would like to see sexual and fertility symbolism in the association of the cat and woman, and a reference to the goddess Hathor. This cannot be excluded, and the Egyptian artist often surprises us by the complexity of his design and the richness of ideas which it contains. Certainly, the cat's association with some aspects of Hathor was at this time established. Nevertheless, a completely convincing proof is difficult to find. Cats have, of course, been linked with sexual and fertility images in many cultures, and their ability to reproduce is legendary. Early in the second century AD, Plutarch wrote, rather enigmatically and perhaps mainly in reference to the cat's moon associations, that the Egyptian cat gives birth first to one kitten, then two, three until the number seven is reached, making the total the same as the twenty-eight days of the lunar month.

If the cat under a woman's chair is a sexual and fertility symbol, a similar interpretation should be applied to the dog or the monkey under the man's chair. The monkey's sexual prowess is well-known and was recognized as such by the Egyptians. This is made quite obvious by some of the objects on which the monkey motif is used (e.g. the shape of the containers to hold

34 A monkey and a cat embracing a goose, under the throne of Tiy, the queen of Amenhotep III (1391–1353 BC), as shown in the unfortunately damaged tomb-painting of Anen at Sheikh Abd el-Qurna (Thebes).

35 A spitting 'cat under the chair,' enjoying a less than amicable relationship with a goose, in the tomb of Penbuy and Kasa at Deir el-Medina, c.1250 BC.

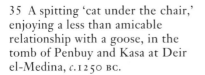

60

36 A girl-servant attending to guests in a banquet scene, with an optimistic long-tailed 'cat under the chair.' The Theban tomb of Nebamun and Ipuky, c.1360 BC.

kohl), but there is nothing in the treatment of these animals in Theban tombs which points to the same idea. If such symbolism is present, it is very subtle. A variation of the 'cat under the chair' theme also occurs in banquet scenes.

The cat is only a very small element, whether symbolically charged or not, in these artistic compositions and its importance does not exceed that of a minor motif which conveniently fills a rather awkward empty space. Nevertheless, the mere fact that it appears suggests that the animal's presence in the house was now taken for granted. The treatment of the cat displays some lovingly humorous touches. Under the throne of Tiy, the queen of Amenhotep III (1391–1353 BC), represented in the tomb of their contemporary Anen (TT 120), there is a monkey and a most unlikely pair seemingly in a passionate embrace: a cat and a large goose. The same theme was taken up in the approximately contemporary tomb of Ramose (TT 55) and the already mentioned Ramesside tomb of Ipuy (TT 217), but the bird is now much smaller than the cat. In the Ramesside tomb of Penbuy and Kasa (TT 10) the cat and the goose seem well matched; the cat is not necessarily going to be the winner of that particular confrontation. A monkey and a cat appear together on several occasions, the former under the chair of the man, the latter under that of the wife, e.g. in the Ramesside (after c.1295 BC) tombs

37 (*Left*) A cat gnawing a bone under the chair of wife Mutemwia, on a painting in the tomb of Neferronpet Kenro, *c.*1250 BC.

38 (*Right*) A picture of anxiety. A cat tied to the ornamental leg of a chair and apparently unable to reach its bowl filled with meat. Painting in the tomb of May, *c.*1450 BC.

39 (*Right, below*) A 'cat under the chair' of Tawi, the wife of Nakht, on a wall-painting in his tomb at Sheikh Abd el-Qurna, probably of the reign of Thutmose IV (1401–1391 BC).

of Raya (TT 159) and Penne Sunero (TT 331). Fights between the two pets must have been a sight to behold and there is little doubt about which of the animals was the artist's favourite in the tomb of Neferhotep (TT 50), of the reign of Horemheb (1323–1295 BC). The cat, its face shown in front view, seems to have taken the monkey by complete surprise and appears to be carried by it in a piggyback fashion: it has one of its front paws on the monkey's head and the hind paws firmly on its back.

Perhaps not surprisingly, the majority of the cats in Theban tombs are demonstrating their incomparable opportunism as they are busily feeding. The object of their attention may be a large leg-bone with meat placed in a bowl or basket, as in the tomb of Sennufer (TT 96), of the reign of Amenhotep II (1427–1401 BC), or only slightly less sumptuous meals in the Ramesside tombs of Raya (TT 159) and Neferronpet Kenro (TT 178). In the tomb of May (TT 130), probably dated to the reign of Thutmose III (1479–

1425 BC), the cat is tied to the leg of the chair with a red ribbon, and there is a bowl filled with pieces of meat nearby but apparently just out of the anxious animal's reach. The cat in the tomb of Nakht (TT 52), probably of the reign of Thutmose IV (1401–1391 BC), is eating a large fish. The cat's arched back and its stretched front paws, firmly holding the fish down as it voraciously attacks it, wonderfully convey the feeling of compressed animal energy and the cat's excitement at such a feast. A variation on the same theme exists, sketched on a small limestone flake, and reminds us that a sole occurrence in tomb decoration need not guarantee originality. It is worth pointing out that while the protagonist of these scenes may be new, the subject had already been known to Old-Kingdom artists. In the tomb of Nika-ankh at Tihna, in Middle Egypt, which dates to c.2450 BC, there is a dog under his master's chair busily eating a goose.

Whenever it can be ascertained, the colour of the coat of the cats in Theban tombs is fairly uniformly somewhere between sandy yellow and light reddish brown. The markings of the fur are indicated either by dark stippling or by longer brushstrokes, but both techniques suggest a pattern which we would associate with striped tabbies. The animal thus very much resembles the wild cat, *Felis silvestris libyca*. This is in agreement with the evidence gleaned from the examination of cat mummies; most of those are, of course, Ptolemaic, i.e. some 1000 years later.

A cat under the chair of the wife can also be seen on several stelae (grave-

40 A 'cat under the chair' on a fragment of a stela, probably from the Theban area and dating to c.1450 BC. Florence, Museo Archeologico.

41 Simut fowling in the marshes, accompanied by his wife, children and the family cat. A Theban tomb-painting of the 14th century BC, copied by Sir J. Gardner Wilkinson.

stones) which are approximately contemporary with the Theban tombs described above.

The motif of the cat under the chair was not confined to tomb decoration or to stelae. A real, highly decorative gilt chair, found in the tomb of Yuiu and Tjuiu, the parents of Tiy who was the wife of Amenhotep III (1391–1353 BC), displays a scene showing the queen in a papyrus skiff during what looks like a pleasure cruise in the marshes. Princess Satamun is offering her a bouquet, and another princess is standing behind her. Under the chair of the seated queen there is a large tabby cat. Apotropaic creatures and beings, about which I shall talk later, appear on the carved armrests of the chair. This is an interesting link between the formal domestic scenes with the tomb owner accompanied by his wife, and the traditional marsh-scenes in which he is hunting birds and spearing fish. We have already seen from the much earlier Saqqara tomb of Princess Seshseshet Idut that when a woman was required to take the leading role in such a scene the composition was modified in favour of a more leisurely pursuit.

At least half a dozen scenes of hunting birds and spearing fish which include cats may be found in Theban tombs; others may have escaped my attention or have not been published. They are those of Amenemhat (TT 53, of the reign of Thutmose III, 1479–1425 BC), Nebamun (probably of the same date), Kenamun (TT 93, of the reign of Amenhotep II, 1427–1401 BC), Menna

42 Nebamun, accompanied by the family cat, on an imaginary hunting trip in the marshes.
A Theban tomb painting of *c.*1450 BC or a little later. British Museum.

(TT 69, probably the reigns of Thutmose IV or Amenhotep III, 1401–
1353 BC), Simut (TT A.24, the reign of Amenhotep III, 1391–1353 BC), and
again of the Ramesside Ipuy (TT 217). It is clear that either Ipuy or the artist
who was responsible for the decoration of his tomb must have been a great
cat-lover, because the animal occurs there in three different scenes. Misunderstanding based on a naively literal interpretation of marsh scenes has led
some scholars to suggest that these provide evidence that the cat was used
by the Egyptians for retrieving. A modified view concedes that the proposition
seems unlikely but would like to see cats used to flush fowl out of their hiding
places. The theory is seemingly quite attractive. The birds would rise swiftly
on the hunter's approach and so would not give him more than a fleeting

66

43 Nebamun's cat going frantic among birds hunted in the marshes by its owner (detail of fig.42), *c*.1450 BC or a little later. British Museum.

moment in which to launch his throwstick. They would, however, instinctively try to protect their nests against a cat and so present the hunter with
more targets. We have seen that the ichneumon may have earlier been
employed for the same purpose.

The cat was a new element in the old genre of hunting scenes and the
artists incorporated it in different ways. In the tomb of Amenemhat the cat
is climbing a single papyrus stalk which bends under its weight as the animal
strives to reach a nest with three eggs. This, we have seen, was how the
ichneumon and the genet used to be shown in Old-Kingdom tombs. The
cat, however, appears to have been left unfinished or the design was altered.
The yellow-brown fur of Menna's cat has the dorsal line indicated by a series
of heavy dark dots and the stripes by dark vertical brushstrokes. It skips
nimbly from one papyrus umbel to another while the cat of Ipuy seems to
scramble upwards laboriously in very much the same way as the genets in
the Middle-Kingdom tomb of Khnumhotep III at Beni Hasan. Ipuy's cat has
a thick dark line along its back, with the tabby pattern shown by series of
dots arranged in horizontal lines. The cat of Simut, an animal with a striped
coat and a ringed tail, stands on its hind legs and with its front paws clings
to the long kilt of its master, as if attempting to reach the decoy bird in the
hunter's left hand.

It is, I suspect, Nebamun's cat which has caused the confusion about
'retrieving.' It is balancing on two papyrus stalks, with one small bird grasped
in the claws of its front paws, another under its hind paws, and its sharp teeth
sunk into the wing of a third, a duck. The hairs of its light brown coat are
indicated by stippling; the stripes are suggested by soft dark lines running
horizontally like necklaces across its throat and chest, and by less sharply
defined vertical lines on the body. Its tail is black-tipped with two dark rings.
The representation of Nebamun's cat is curiously 'un-Egyptian' and, viewed
in isolation, would easily pass for a European animal painting. The composition of the scene is superb and worth examining in greater detail. Nebamun
is standing in a small papyrus canoe, holding three decoy birds in his right
hand, and poised to hurl a serpent-shaped throwing stick which he grasps in
his left hand. He wears a short wig. Round his neck there is an ornamental
broad collar of multiple strands of beads. Three stalks with a lotus flower
and two buds are casually thrown over his shoulder. Round his hips Nebamun
wears a short pleated kilt. His wife, dressed up in all her finery, is standing
primly behind him holding a bouquet of flowers, a *menat*-necklace and a
sistrum (ceremonial rattle). Nebamun's small daughter is kneeling at her
father's feet, clinging to the calf of his left leg with her right hand and
plucking a bunch of lotus flowers with her left hand. This is, of course,
another example of a clever artistic device to fill the space between Nebamun's

feet. There is a duck in the prow of the boat. The birds in the papyrus clumps are represented as a *mélange* of wings and beaks. Beautifully observed butterflies beat their wings wherever there is enough room; one of them is about to settle on Nebamun's left foot. I should mention in passing that, perhaps not surprisingly, some scholars see deep erotic symbolism in these marsh scenes. Symbolism in art is extremely difficult to prove or disprove, and as this would take us far away from cats, I do not propose to examine this particular approach in detail.

Nebamun's cat looks so much at home in the scene of the hunt in the marshes that it looks as though cats have always been part of it. 'At home' is a clue to its inclusion here and elsewhere. The cat was now regarded as an integral element of 'family at home' scenes and its presence was felt necessary even in the imaginary marsh scenes. The tomb owner was accompanied by his family and the occasion would not have been the same without the family pet. At this point reality began to intrude upon the fictitious world. Since the scene was a wild bird hunt, the artist showed the cat reacting to the situation the way it would have in the real world. This, however, provides no serious grounds for the theory that it was employed for retrieving. The question is not whether the Egyptian cat could or could not have been trained to perform this task. There is just no evidence to support the proposition.

The 'cat in the marshes' motif continued to appear sporadically even after the end of the New Kingdom. The Theban tomb of Montuemhat (TT 34), dated to *c*.650 BC, has already been mentioned, and there is a cat in the only slightly later marsh-scene of Patjenfy from Heliopolis.

Thebes was not the only necropolis of importance during the New Kingdom. For reasons of economic and administrative convenience Memphis became the capital of Egypt sometime around 1450 BC, if not earlier, although Thebes retained its religious importance. For quite a long time, tombs built in the main Memphite necropolis could not compete in the quality of their decoration with their Theban counterparts. At first, the larger tombs were made in the poor-quality rock at Saqqara. The earliest free-standing tomb-chapel decorated in relief belongs to a treasury official, Mery-mery, who was a contemporary of Amenhotep III (1391–1353 BC). In his chapel the cat appears, in its 'hieroglyphic' image but with one of the front paws raised, under the chair of his wife Meryt-ptah. Shortly after this tomb had been completed, King Amenhotep IV (1353–1337 BC) initiated the greatest religious upheaval pharaonic Egypt knew. Only one deity, the impersonal Aten (portrayed as a sun disc with its rays terminated in human hands), began to be preferred early in the king's reign. The traditional pantheon was mainly ignored. The king changed his name to Akhenaten ('Radiance of the Aten') and transferred his residence to the newly founded city of Akhetaten ('Horizon of the Aten') at Amarna (hence the term 'Amarna period') in Middle Egypt, near modern Ashmunein. The old gods and their temples and priests were at first ignored and eventually actively persecuted.

The decoration of the temples hastily put up for the worship of the new deity was full of interesting and previously unseen features, but the cat appeared neither in the bustling activities around the royal palaces and their storehouses nor in the more official scenes. The same fate befell the other pet animals such as dogs and monkeys. The art of the Amarna period is full of prancing caparisoned horses and speeding chariots, dashing soldiers and grovelling officials, endless ceremonies in front of the Aten's altars, and the publicly-vaunted domestic happiness of the royal family, but despite the undeniable beauty of some of its masterpieces it is not a homely and cosy art, and the cats probably did not fit in. It may also be that their association, at that time modest at best, and those of other animals, with some of the proscribed deities contributed to their exclusion. Be that as it may, when the Amarna regime collapsed after the death of Akhenaten, his second successor expurgated the name of the Aten from his own name, changed it to Tutankhamun, and moved his royal residence back to Memphis. The Amarna artists who arrived in the Memphite area now inspired an unprecedented upsurge in the standard of tomb decoration. The cat, however, hardly appears. New-Kingdom tombs dating from this period at Memphis are as yet little known and it is, of course, possible that scenes with cats are still waiting to be discovered under the Saqqara sand. We have, however, already seen that the inclusion of the cat was very much a solution to a specific artistic problem, that of space, chosen by Theban artists. It seems that the Amarna-inspired Memphite school of tomb decoration preferred other motifs, such as children and monkeys, instead. It would be rash to draw conclusions based on negative evidence, so for the time being it must suffice if we accept that the precise reasons for the scarcity of cats in New-Kingdom tombs at Memphis are not yet known.

During the New Kingdom (1540–1069 BC) the cat appeared on decorative items or objects of daily use where the reasons for its inclusion were primarily aesthetic. Nevertheless, ideological (religious) connotations were never far away. A broad collar of Queen Ahhotep, the wife of King Seqenenra Taa II (1571–1556 BC), contained eighteen small gold pendants in the shape of seated cats. Bead armlets with gold bars with inlaid gold, carnelian and faience figures of recumbent cats, each with its front paws crossed and its head turned, were found in the tomb of the three wives of Thutmose III (1479–1425 BC) at Thebes. It seems that the motif of cats was used on the jewellery of queens in the same way as sphinxes (human-headed lions) were on the personal ornaments of kings.

44 A 'cat under the chair' at Saqqara, on a relief from the tomb of Mery-Mery, a contemporary of Amenhotep III (1391–1353 BC). Leiden, Rijksmuseum van Oudheden.

Egyptian hand-held mirrors were large, brightly-polished copper discs. Their handles varied considerably but one type was carved in wood in the form of a nude girl holding a small cat. The handle was originally gilded. The mirror was, of course, one of the items associated with the goddess Hathor, and we shall describe her connection with the cat later. For some, this explains the presence of the cat on mirror handles.

This may be the right place to mention briefly the role the cat played in Egyptian medicine, famous throughout the ancient world, and in practical household matters. The fat, fur, and excrement of the tomcat, and the placenta and fur of the female cat, appear in prescriptions, luckily used exclusively externally or in fumigation. Some of these should not be allowed to fall into oblivion. The fat of a tomcat smeared over things was guaranteed to keep the mice away. A remedy for relieving stiffness in various parts of the body was to apply a bandage with a mixture of animal (pig, snake, an unidentified *ibtjersu* creature, mouse, and cat) fats. A cat placenta was an important element in a lotion which prevented hair from going grey; unfortunately, there are no instructions on whether it was sufficient to apply it only when the person was out of the public eye or whether it had to be worn for a longer period of time for the preparation to be effective. A female cat's fur mixed with human milk and resin was put on burns, accompanied by the recitation of an appropriate spell.

Large decorated tombs were still built at Saqqara during the reign of Ramses IV (1153–1147 BC), but it was the Delta which was now commanding attention as the stage on which Egypt's destiny was going to unfold. For its part, the cat, having secured acceptance in Egyptian houses, was about to make a decisive bid for a place in the Egyptian pantheon.

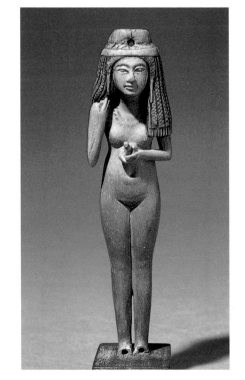

45 A wooden figure of a nude girl carrying a kitten, probably the decorative handle of an object such as a mirror. Probably from Thebes, *c.*1370 BC. British Museum.

A poor man's lion
The divine cats

The progress of the cat in Egyptian religion was quite remarkable and in many respects unusual. Unlike some other animals, the cat did not appear in the right place at the right time, and was not prominently associated with an important local deity at the beginning of Egyptian history. It never attained a truly elevated 'official' status which would have enabled it to become a full member of the divine community encountered on the walls of Egyptian temples. We would search there in vain for representations of a cat-headed goddess. In spite of all this, the cat's popularity eventually surpassed that of any other animal and reached far beyond Egypt's boundaries.

The cat's strength lay in its humble origins and its apotropaic (protective) qualities, which first brought it widespread respect and a prominent place in the personal religion of ordinary people. These characteristics soon led to the association of the male cat with the sun-god and the complex of beliefs concerning the sun's night journey through the underworld, so securing it, in religious terms, the highest possible connections. An unexpected twist of history helped the cat early in the first millennium BC when the city of Bubastis (modern Tell Basta, near Zagazig in the eastern Delta) provided some of the rulers for an Egypt which was then struggling through a period of uncertainty and disunity. It appears that the linking of the female cat with the goddess Bastet started at that time. During the Ptolemaic period (332–30 BC) the cat's popularity reached its peak. It was the most Egyptian of all the animals associated with Egyptian gods and one which never lost a certain aura of aloofness and mystery (in this respect the slow beginnings of its domestication paid off handsomely in the end), and was a familiar sight in most houses. Popular religious beliefs, sometimes castigated as 'primitive' because of their emphasis on gods manifesting themselves through animals, proved to possess more vitality than the elaborate and more abstract religious systems of pharaonic Egypt. These ideas were now skilfully manipulated by the state and the temples to their own advantage, and were enthusiastically supported by the vast majority of Egyptians. Was this a sign of failure? Perhaps, and it was certainly evidence of profound ideological re-thinking and re-evaluation. When Christianity reached Egypt, the ground had already been prepared for the disintegration of the old structure.

The spiritual edifice of ancient Egyptian religion may be compared to a real building of brick and mortar. Seen from outside, the façade of an old house which has been lived in for a long time, and has been rebuilt and modified on many occasions, seems deceptively revealing because it is full of windows – big and small, old and new, some shuttered or boarded up, others flung open. But their large number, their different shapes and sizes, and the absence of a single pattern may confuse rather than help the viewer. We learn only a little about the rooms behind the façade, still less about their mutual relationship and the interior layout of the house, and nothing about the rooms which have no windows at all. In the same way, our understanding of ancient Egyptian religion may be made difficult by the number of its deities and their individual characteristics, but even more so by the complexity of their relationships, the multi-layered composition of the whole structure, and the reticence of our sources about some of its aspects.

Ancient Egyptian religion was a vast and largely unsystematic collection of diverse ideological beliefs which developed in different parts of the country in prehistoric times, before 3000 BC, and which continued to be modified and changed throughout Egyptian history by the inter-action of various elements and the inclusion of new ones. The fluctuating fortunes of Egyptian cities such as Henen-nesu (Heracleopolis, modern Ihnasya el-Medina), Weset (Thebes, Luxor), and Per-Bastet (Bubastis, Tell Basta) had a direct bearing on the standing of their local deities (Harsaphes, Amun, Bastet). There were partial efforts to order ideas concerning deities of the most important religious centres, such as On (Heliopolis, a suburb of Cairo), Mennufer (Memphis, south-west of Cairo) and Khemenu (Hermopolis, Ashmunein in Middle Egypt), but there were no attempts to introduce a uniform system for the whole country. This must be regarded as unusual in a society where the king held such a uniquely centralized position; one would expect this to have been reflected in religion.

The term 'religion' covered a wider area in ancient Egypt than the more limited sense in which we understand it nowadays. It also included ideas which we describe differently, such as state ideology and the theory of king-ship, concerned with the position of the king and his relationship to gods. The complex religious ideas expressed in the texts and decoration of Egyptian temples were the ideological property of the minority; only priests associated with these temples would have been able to read the inscriptions and see the representations in any case. The majority of people were not allowed beyond the temple's monumental gateway (pylon). Egyptian temples were not places where religious dogmas would have been spread among and affirmed by ordinary people. There was a large diversity of religious feelings within vari-ous sections of Egyptian society: personal beliefs of the owners of large decorated tombs were not the same as the religion of the poor. This further deepened the differences in Egyptian society because many of the high officials also held priestly functions. It seems that there were hardly any full-time priests before the beginning of the Middle Kingdom (c.2040 BC).

Different religious 'levels' did not remain fixed and isolated; there was a certain amount of interchange between them. Even the humblest peasant, who would have had no understanding of the religious concepts conveyed by the scenes on the walls of Egyptian temples, could be present when the temple image was brought out and carried in procession during religious festivals. The beliefs of the poor, which usually went unrecorded, were sometimes 'promoted' and received official recognition so that they became part of the religion, recorded in some detail in sources available to us. Modern Egyptological analysis distinguishes four main 'dimensions' of ancient Egyptian religion. The first three belong to the restricted 'official' sphere, such as beliefs concerning local deities and their temples, cosmic events and the maintenance of the existing order in the universe, nature and society, and primitive mythology; religious beliefs of individuals ('personal piety') represent the fourth 'dimension.'

The piety of the Egyptians impressed all visitors from abroad, but the role animals played in their religion was one of the most misunderstood aspects of the country. The situation was best summed up by the mistaken statement of Herodotus that all animals were held sacred. Foreigners were fascinated (some repelled) by this aspect of Egyptian culture. Clement of Alexandria, a militant Christian writer of the second century AD, was openly scathing about the Egyptian gods being 'a cat or a crocodile, or a native snake or a similar animal, which should not be in a temple, but in a cleft or a den or on a dung heap' (translation K. A. D. Smelik). Some of the recorded evidence concerning the Egyptians and animals is anecdotal but conveys the character of the period the better for it. Herodotus wrote that when an Egyptian house was on fire, its inhabitants were more concerned about the fate of their cats than their possessions. At the time of his visit to Egypt, sometime in the mid-fifth century BC, even household cats were regarded as manifestations of a deity and his statement must be seen in this light. He also adds, rather perplexingly, that in such a situation the cats 'leap over the men and spring into the fire.' Should this be explained by the maternal instinct of female cats trying to rescue their kittens? Or is it a rather distorted comment on the cat's love of warmth? In the second century AD, the Macedonian rhetorician Polyaenus gave an account of the battle of Pelusium, in the eastern Delta, in 525 BC. The stratagem of the Persian conqueror Cambyses was to shield his soldiers from missiles by putting rows of animals, cats among them, in the front rank. The Egyptians were afraid that they might injure or kill their gods and duly lost the battle. It is unlikely, though, that this is a true story. Cambyses acquired a bad reputation as far as Egyptian religion was concerned. According to Herodotus, he was responsible for mortally wounding the Apis-bull at Memphis, a crime which must have been so heinous that there was no punishment available for it.

In a country like Egypt, animal forms were easily understood and required no further explanation because they were part of everybody's daily experience. The division which we instinctively make between people and animals was not so strongly felt and the category 'animals' did not, in fact, exist. To put it differently, 'living beings' included gods, people, and animals. A theological treatise recorded under Shabako (716–702 BC) but perhaps composed as early as the third millennium BC, describes the heart and tongue of the creator-god Ptah being present in 'all gods, all people, all cattle, all worms, all that lives.' Just like people, animals were made by the creator god, worshipped him (in their own way) and were looked after by him. In certain exceptional cases, their link with the god may have even been more immediate than that of humans.

Images were very significant in all aspects of Egyptian culture but nowhere more so than in religion. A deity was worshipped in its visible epiphany (manifestation), as a cult image. These could be of various types, either inanimate (statues or two-dimensional representations of deities, heavenly bodies, exceptionally even objects) or live animals. An animal was chosen to act as a god's image for the period of its natural life because of its special external characteristics, such as an unusual pattern of markings on the hide of the Apis-bull at Memphis. It was unique and when it died, it was buried as befitted its status and a successor was selected. The role of animals in Egyptian religion was quite different from, and had nothing to do with, zoolatry (animal worship), and to talk about 'deification' of cats misses the point.

In temples, an image was the focus of the ritual performed there regularly. These were almost private affairs. In theory only the king took part, but in practice the priests, as his deputies, acted on his behalf. The rest of the population was excluded. Egyptian art contributed to the confusion of outsiders by introducing hybrid forms of representations of deities in which human bodies were combined with animal heads, but these had no special religious value of their own and were purely artistic devices.

Several animals could be regarded as manifestations of the same deity. The god Amun of Thebes could manifest himself in the shape of the ram or the goose, or Thoth of Hermopolis as the baboon or the ibis. The same animal species could be associated with deities at several different localities. There were bull cults such as that of Apis at Memphis, Mnevis at Heliopolis, Buchis at Hermonthis (modern Armant, south of Luxor), and others at various Delta sites. The ram was the animal of the gods Khnum of Elephantine (near Aswan, in the first Nile cataract area) and Amun, and was also important at Mendes (Tell el-Ruba, in the central Delta) as the 'Ram Lord of Djedet (= Mendes).' Cult images of the same deity could be anthropomorphic (imitating human beings) as well as zoomorphic (imitating animals). The fact that a deity could manifest itself in the form of an animal did not preclude that animal's economic exploitation (cattle are a case in point) and did not mean that all members of the species were regarded in the same way. However, relatives of the animal chosen as the god's cult image (e.g. the mother of the Apis-bull and his offspring) may have been treated in a special way.

The number of animals regarded as manifestations of a deity increased enormously towards the end of pharaonic history and in Ptolemaic and Roman Egypt. Hor, a priest in the temple at Abydos sometime during the third century BC, proudly proclaimed 'I have provided food for the ibis, the falcon, the cat, and the jackal.' The concept was extended to cover domestic animals, such as cats, perhaps dogs, snakes and some birds. In a way, there was a god present even in the humblest Egyptian household.

At first, the cat was very much a minor auxiliary figure on the periphery of religious beliefs and had to 'prove' itself at every stage of its rise to prominence. It does not appear in the oldest corpus of Egyptian religious spells, the *Pyramid Texts*, so called because they were inscribed on the walls of rooms and corridors of royal pyramids between about 2340 BC and the end of the Old Kingdom, some two hundred years later. The purpose of these texts was to equip the deceased king with spells he might need to overcome difficulties in his other existence.

In the *Pyramid Texts*, a cat-like goddess called Mafdet (perhaps 'Runner') is described as killing a serpent with her claws. Fortunately, we have a representation of the animal, identified by an inscription, on a stone vase of c.2950–2800 BC, found in a royal tomb at Abydos and so we know that this was a larger cat, probably the leopard (*Panthera pardus*) or cheetah (*Acinonyx jubatus*). The latter is probably the fastest land-creature on earth and its Egyptian name would be very appropriate. At the beginning of Egyptian history, such animals would have been tamed and kept in the royal palace for companionship, protection and prestige. The custom did not seem to have been kept up and another big cat, the lion, became more prominently associated with royalty in the Old Kingdom (after 2647 BC). Later, there are instances of lions kept as the king's pet animals shortly before and during the Ramesside period (from c.1330 BC). This, however, was not the last appearance of the goddess Mafdet who, as a deity manifesting herself in the form of a 'panther' embodying the qualities of big cats, continued to appear sporadically throughout the rest of Egyptian history. As we shall see later, she may have been the first goddess represented as a cat-headed woman.

The earliest representations of the cat in a religious context seem to have been on the so-called magic knives which were an important part of tomb equipment during the Middle Kingdom, from around 2000 BC till about 1500 BC. They need not have been purely funerary; some may have been used in their owner's lifetime. The magic knives are curved, narrow and flat objects, usually made of hippopotamus ivory, and vaguely resemble large ceremonial flint knives. Their incised decoration shows a series of animals and curious creatures and beings, demigods rather than gods: lions and snakes with knives, long-tailed dwarfs with leonine faces, serpent-headed beings with human bodies, long-necked animals resembling giraffes but initially perhaps based on the appearance of the cheetah, pregnant hippopotami with crocodiles on their back, bird-headed griffins with a human head on their withers, turtles, frogs and beetles, and also cats. These were the nightmarish inhabitants of the world of popular beliefs rather than representatives of the religion of temple walls, the lesser gods rather than full members of the pantheon. The purpose of these objects was apotropaic, to provide protection against the prosaic dangers of everyday existence, such as scorpions and poisonous snakes, but also illnesses and accidents, difficult births, nightmares and fear of the unknown. Most of them, it seems, belonged to women and children. The cat was, no doubt, included because of its ability to destroy snakes, in the role assigned in the *Pyramid Texts* to the goddess Mafdet.

The cat could be shown in its 'hieroglyphic' image, sometimes with one paw raised wielding a large knife. This was the traditional Egyptian instrument for 'cutting off the heads' of enemies, a custom recorded in a most vivid way on the palette of King Narmer (*c.*2975 BC). Originally such palettes, usually slabs of slate, were functional and employed for the grinding of materials used in eye make-up. Later they became highly decorative ceremonial or votive objects. 'Cutting off the heads' must have been carried out with a flint knife,

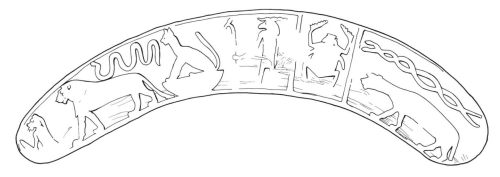

46 An ivory magic knife of *c.*1850 BC. Among the protective creatures are a hippopotamus with a knife, a lion, a cat on a basket, and a 'panther.' British Museum.

but there is no suggestion that it was still practised in pharaonic Egypt. The image, in a way, reflected an old-fashioned figure of speech and collective memory. Iconographically remarkable are representations of cats standing on their hind paws and holding such a knife in both front paws.

The cat is mentioned in a similar role in the *Coffin Texts*. These began to be written on wooden coffins from about 2100 BC and performed the same role for ordinary people as the *Pyramid Texts* did earlier for the kings. In Spell 335, the deceased declares: 'I am the Great Tomcat (*miu oa*) which split the *ished*-tree on its side in On (= Heliopolis, the home-town of the sun-god) on the night of making war and warding off the rebels, and on the day of destroying the foes of the Lord of All.' The *ished*-tree was the sacred tree of the sun-god at Heliopolis but the precise significance of its 'splitting,' perhaps in order to allow the sun to rise, is not clear. The text continues: 'Who is this Great Tomcat? He is the god Ra himself. He was called "cat" (*miu*) when Sia (= personification of knowledge) spoke of him because he was mewing during what he was doing, and that was how his name of "cat" came into being.' We learn two important things: the male cat is clearly linked with the sun-god as his supporter and his manifestation, and the etymology of the word for 'cat' is given here. A reference to the 'cry of a tomcat' is made in the *Book of Amduat*, which I shall mention later, where it is compared with the voices of the souls of the inhabitants of the underworld. In the *Coffin Texts* the word 'cat' is sometimes written with a taxogram (a sign indicating a category) of a 'hieroglyphic' cat.

The nature of the cat and some of its characteristics ensured that it figured prominently in superstitions. According to one of the earliest dream-books which contains interpretations of dreams, perhaps compiled as early as *c.*1980–1801 BC, if a man sees himself in a dream 'seeing a large cat (*mii oa*),' it is a good omen, and means that 'a large harvest will come to him.' From what I have said about the connection between farmers and cats, it seems that there is some logic present in this. A similar demotic composition, of the second century AD, describes a situation in which one meets a cat, but the text is too fragmentary to establish its significance.

Apotropaic demons, including cats, may occasionally occur on various objects of daily use, such as cosmetic jars. Small amulets showing cats, in bone or green faience, were found in the cemeteries in the Qaw – Badari area of Upper Egypt, and dated to the end of the Old Kingdom and the First Intermediate Period (between *c.*2300 and 2040 BC). Worn on the body or clothes, they would have provided a round-the-clock protection against the hazards of everyday life.

The apotropaic function of the cat was never entirely lost. It still appears in this original role, as a protective animal, on small amulet-stelae ('cippi') and 'magic' statues of the Late, Ptolemaic and Roman periods. They functioned in a way which was similar to that of magic knives, with special emphasis on protection against snake-bites and scorpion-stings. On one such stela, made during the reign of Nectanebo II (360–342 BC), a distressed female cat who has been stung by a scorpion appeals to the sun-god to come and help 'his daughter.' The sun-god calms her down and assures her that it is in his power to render the poison ineffective and promises her his protection.

In the meantime, however, the cat had moved on to greater things in what could be described as the second stage of its rise to religious prominence. Royal tombs of the New Kingdom (after 1540 BC) in the Valley of the Kings contained on their walls copies of the so-called underworld books. These were texts and representations which described and portrayed in detail the dark watery underworld region into which the sun-god Ra had to descend at the end of every day and which he traversed during the night. The tomb walls acted as huge sheets of papyrus from which these compositions were

47 Detail of painted decoration of the coffin of Djedhorefankh, showing several forms of the sun-god, from Deir el-Bahri, c.900 BC. British Museum.

copied; the background colour of these texts is that of a page of a papyrus scroll. The journey was fraught with danger and difficulties and many obstacles put in the sun-god's way had to be overcome and numerous enemies trying to hinder his progress had to be defeated before the nightly sojourn was over and the sun could triumphantly re-appear on the eastern horizon at dawn. Various demon-helpers facilitated the journey, among them cats and cat-headed beings. They were the same motley crew we have already met on magic knives.

In the *Book of Amduat* ('The Book of What is in the Underworld') a demon 'of brutal face', represented cat-headed or at least with a cat's ears, is seen decapitating bound enemies in a scene reminiscent of the traditional triumphant scene featuring the pharaoh. This may have once had some basis in reality but, contrary to the opinion of some Egyptologists, it is extremely unlikely that such a barbaric act would have been publicly performed in pharaonic Egypt. In the *Book of the Caverns* a cat-headed demon called Miuty

48 Different forms of the sun-god, including one which is cat-headed, painted on the anthropoid coffin of Amenemope, from Thebes, c.900 BC. British Museum.

(from *miu*, 'cat') is shown watching over bound enemies of the sun-god, and in the *Book of the Gates* the porter, also called Miuty, who guards the last gate through which the sun-god must pass, is cat-headed and holds two sceptres. One of these is serpent-shaped. After the end of the New Kingdom (1069 BC), the texts and vignettes of these 'underworld books' began to be copied on coffins of ordinary people.

Finally, the sun-god could manifest himself in the form of the cat. In the *Litany of the Sun*, which enumerates his seventy-five names and his corresponding seventy-four forms, he appears as such twice: as Miuty and as the 'Great Tomcat' (*miu oa*). A remarkable representation of a seated cat appears on one of the pillars in the burial chamber of Thutmose III (1479–1425 BC). The animal, which was sketched with maximum economy, has a ringed tail and tabby body markings indicated by series of semi-circular dashes. A cat-headed form of the sun-god appears on the second gold shrine of Tutankhamun (1336–1327 BC). For some three hundred years after the end of the New Kingdom, until about the middle of the eighth century BC, some of the forms of the sun-god, including the cat-headed Miuty, were painted on the interior of coffins.

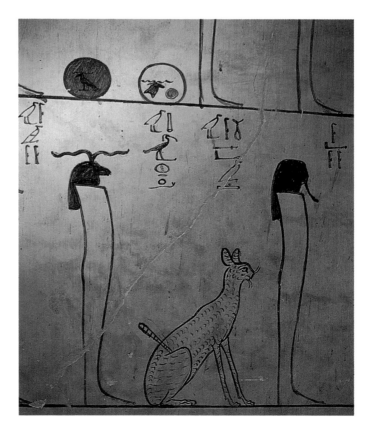

49 A cat representing one of the forms of the sun-god, in a remarkably fluent sketch in the tomb of Thutmose III (1479–1425 BC) in the Valley of the Kings.

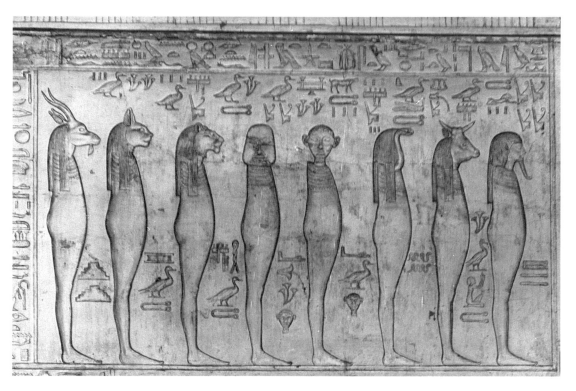

50 Underworld deities or forms of the sun-god, on the second shrine of Tutankhamun (1336–1327 BC). Cairo, Egyptian Museum.

In the papyrus of Nespaheran, an 'oblationer of the temple of the god Amun' probably around 900 BC, the deceased appeals to the 'female cat (*miit*) of lapis lazuli,' a rather leonine looking creature which may be associated with the sun-god because of the epithet 'of the horizon.' Intriguingly, the cat is also described as 'mistress of the embalming house,' perhaps because the original role of the animal was to accompany and serve the sun-god in the underworld, the realm of the dead presided over by the god Osiris.

The ideas contained in the 'underworld books' soon began to be reflected in private tombs and their funerary equipment. A deceased person now hoped to participate in the daily regeneration of the sun-god by associating with him during his nightly journey. During the New Kingdom, religious spells called by Egyptologists the *Book of the Dead* came to be regarded as essential for the tomb owner's well-being in the other world. Illustrated copies of the *Book of the Dead* written on papyri were put in the tomb and also started being inscribed on tomb walls. Some of the imagery is similar to that of the other underworld books. The name formed a part of one's personality and so knowledge of it was all-important. In Spell 145 of the *Book of the Dead* the deceased addresses the twelfth of the gates through which he has to pass as follows: 'The name of the god who guards you is Cat (*mii*).' The guardian of the gate is cat-headed.

The cat appears in the vignette (illustration) accompanying Spell 17 which is closely related to the earlier Spell 335 of the *Coffin Texts*. He is shown killing the sun-god's foe, represented by a serpent. A successful outcome of this confrontation ensured that the sun re-appeared the following morning and that the world continued to function. The cat is usually shown trampling on the serpent with one of its front paws; the other is raised, often holding a knife with which it is about to sever the serpent's head. This subject continued to be represented in copies of the *Book of the Dead* well into the Ptolemaic period (332–30 BC).

In most cases the vignette shows a male cat. There is, however, at least one example where the cat slaying the Apophis snake is female, with clearly indicated teats. This is on a pictorial 'mythological' papyrus of the songstress of the god Amun-Ra, king-of-the-gods, Taudjatre, dated to *c*.1000 BC. The scene is described as 'The killing of the snake Apophis by the living cat who has come out of the underworld and who makes one prosperous in the necropolis.' Since the cat was identified with the deceased person it was, quite logically, shown as female.

This theme is represented in the wall-paintings of several Ramesside tombs (after 1295 BC) at Deir el-Medina, an area of the Theban necropolis where the cat motif appears unusually often. These are no pussycats but strong and powerful animals, and the contrast between them and the barrel-shaped creature under the wife's chair, sporting a necklace and large earrings, in the approximately contemporary tomb of Penbuy and Kasa (TT 10), could hardly be greater. There is a strong likelihood that the prototype of these cats of the sun-god was not the domesticated *Felis silvestris libyca*, but its wild and untamed cousin, the serval (*Felis serval*). It is also remarkable how leonine these cats, with their square and blunt faces, look. It is just possible that the development which before long was going to associate the lioness and the female cat as two aspects of the same goddess, Bastet, may have been foreshadowed in the distinction between domesticated cats and these snake-fighting creatures.

The cats in the tomb of Sennedjem (TT 1), of the reign of Sety I (1294–1279 BC), and a slightly later tomb of Nakhtamun (TT 335), have a long tail and a coat with rows of small dark crescents which produce the effect of a very pronounced striped pattern. Nakhtamun's cat is described as 'great cat, a form of the god Ra,' while the snake is 'Apophis, the enemy of Ra.' The cat in the tomb of Inherkha (TT 359), of the reigns of Ramses III and IV (1184–1147 BC), is something different altogether. This is a large bloodthirsty ani-

51 (*Top*) A cat slaying the Apophis serpent in front of the *ished*-tree, from Spell 17 of the *Book of the Dead* of Ani, *c*.1250 BC. British Museum. 52 (*Below*) Another version of the theme, from a papyrus with the *Book of the Dead* of Hunufer, perhaps from Memphis, *c*.1280 BC. British Museum.

53 (*Above*) The cat described as 'mistress of the embalming house' in the papyrus of Nespaheran, *c.*900 BC. Oxford, Bodleian Library.

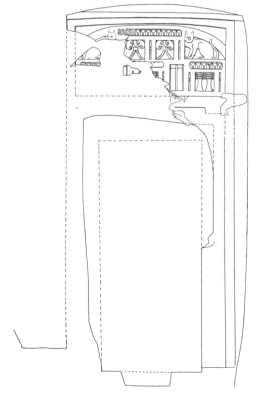

54 (*Left*) Cats as elements of decoration above one of the doorways in the Theban tomb of Amenemhat Surero, of the reign of Amenhotep III (1391–1353 BC).

55 (*Right*) A very strange-looking cat slaying the Apophis snake near the *ished*-tree, in a painting in the Theban tomb of Inherkha, *c.*1160 BC.

mal, with a sandy-coloured coat with very fine spots which, however, do not form any strong pattern, very long and straight ears of which a hare would be proud, and a dark-tipped ringed tail. Its posture is that of a 'hieroglyphic' cat, with its left front paw holding a large knife while the right paw crushes the serpent's head. Blood is spurting from the place where the knife has cut the snake's body. It is difficult to believe that this cat is *Felis silvestris libyca* or even *Felis serval*; one wonders whether the artist tried to show an imaginary cat-like animal and whether the unusual details must be put down to artistic licence.

In Spell 125 there is an interesting reference to an overheard 'conversation which the ass held with the cat;' the cat may represent the sun-god but the role of the ass is unclear. Quite often it stands for his enemy.

The connection of the cat with the sun-god may find its ultimate reflection in *The Hieroglyphics* of Horapollon, an Egyptian author of perhaps the fourth or fifth century AD, who wrote that the animal's pupils changed according to the course of the sun and the time of day, and that at Heliopolis there was a cat-headed xoanon (image) of the god.

An early tendency to associate the cat with the lion may also be reflected in the imitation of decorative screens above the doorways in the tombs of Kenamun (TT 93), of the reign of Amenhotep II (1427–1401 BC), and Amenemhat Surero (TT 48), a contemporary of Amenhotep III (1391–

1353 BC). These devices copy the highly ornamental skylight 'windows' which probably existed in simpler versions in contemporary houses. They are rounded at the top, a form which developed because of the vaulted ceiling of the original room behind such a window, and consist of a combination of decorative motifs known from elsewhere (so-called *djed*-pillars, hawks' heads, papyrus buds, etc.). In real houses they would have formed a latticed grille which allowed in light from outside while protecting the privacy of the room behind it (the principle was developed with consummate skill in the Arab *mashrabiyya*). In these two tombs there are cats seated in the windows. One may wonder whether this is a straightforward record of a common sight or whether we should look for symbolic connotations. The truth may be somewhere in between. The lion had been from the earliest Egyptian history associated with the concept of guardianship, and so representations of these animals or of sphinxes (hybrid forms which combine the lion's body with a human head) are often found in the vicinity of doorways and entrances to temples and palaces. The Great Sphinx which protects the approach to the pyramid-complex of King Khafra (2518–2493 BC) at Giza is the best example. It seems quite likely that the cats in the entablature of the doorways

56 A stela with two cats, and below, the donor and his wife reciting a hymn to the 'great cat' and the sun-god Pre. Probably from Deir el-Medina, *c.*1250 BC or a little later. Oxford, Ashmolean Museum.

in Theban tombs may have had a similar function while at the same time reflecting everyday reality. The motif is also known from some small objects of approximately the same date.

It is because of its connection with the sun-god that the cat appears on some Ramesside stelae found in the Theban area. These monuments belong to the sphere of 'personal piety' and most of them were commissioned by fairly ordinary people, often workmen from Deir el-Medina who would have been able to make them themselves or have them manufactured by their comrades. In certain areas of the large temples of the main national gods, particularly near their entrances, private individuals were allowed to set up small round-topped slabs of stone, 'stelae.' Small shrines, so-called contra-temples, were sometimes specially made at the back of large sanctuaries for the ordinary populace to worship.

A stela may contain a representation of the deity to whom it was presented, with its donor, perhaps accompanied by other members of his family, shown before it or in the register below. The texts are usually short hymns in honour of the deity, and include personal requests which, however, are never too specific. That the cat stands for the sun-god is sometimes made clear by the inscriptions. On one such stela, dated to *c.*1250 BC, there are two rather plump 'hieroglyphic' cats shown in the stela's rounded 'lunette,' one called 'perfect (or young) cat (*miit nufer*) of the god Pre (i.e. Ra, the sun-god),' the other is 'great (or elder) cat (*miit oa*), the peaceful one, in his perfect name of Atum, at peace.' Atum was another name of the sun-god and the contrast between the epithets 'perfect' and 'great' is found often in Egyptian texts. There is a curious mixture of grammatical genders in the description of the cats. This need not be significant at all, but it may be an oblique reference to the sun-god's 'eye' personified by several goddesses, among them Tefnut, Hathor, and Mut. These were regarded as his daughters and most of them could take on the form of a lioness, but such an interpretation would associate the cat with the lioness some three hundred years before such a development can be demonstrated for the goddess Bastet. Underneath, the donor is simultaneously addressing the 'great cat' and the sun-god:

> Giving praise to the great cat,
> kissing the earth before Pre, the great god.
> O peaceful one, who returns to peace,
> you cause me to see the darkness of your making.
> Lighten me that I can perceive your beauty,
> turn towards me,
> o beautiful one when at peace,
> the peaceful one who knows a return to peace.
> May you give life, prosperity, and health
> to the *ka* of . . .

The space for the name of the donor was left blank, probably because this was a monument made in advance and the name was going to be filled in when a prospective buyer was found. These were simple stelae but even so their design and the composition of their texts were quite sophisticated. The texts contains a play on the words *sehedj*, which may mean 'make light' in a physical sense (for example, when describing a dawn, but also when referring to a remedy for a person who suffered from an eye disease) as well as 'instruct,' and we are left to guess which meaning was intended. Also the word *an* can be understood either as 'return,' 'returning,' but also as 'beautiful.' Here the taxogram (generic determinative, a hieroglyphic sign which indicates into which category of meanings the word belongs) makes the intended sense clear but there is little doubt that the linking of the two words is not accidental.

On the stela of the foreman Pashed, of *c.*1290 BC, there is a 'hieroglyphic' cat and a goose, described as '(female) cat, mistress of heaven' and 'good goose of Amun,' and the text below indicates that the cat is an animal associated with

57 A stela dedicated by the draughtsman Nebre of Deir el-Medina, with the 'good swallow' and the 'good cat,' *c.*1250 BC. Turin, Museo Egizio.

Amun's female companion, the goddess Mut. It is probable that the Egyptians connected the name of Mut and the word for the female cat, *miit*, in a kind of false etymology. In what might appear to be a rather mind-twisting development, the goddess Mut could now be thought to have been, as a cat, present at the side of the sun-god during the already mentioned episode of the 'splitting of the *ished*-tree at Heliopolis,' known from the *Coffin Texts* and the *Book of the Dead*. This is alluded to in the text known as the *Mut Ritual*.

A similarity between the word for a female cat (*miit*) and the name of Maet, the goddess of truth and order, may explain an interesting feature found on some late bronze statuettes of cats. Some of them display a figure of the goddess as an element of a necklace round the animal's neck, or Maet's symbol, an ostrich feather, was used to imitate the pattern of the fine hairs inside the cat's ears.

Some monuments do not make it obvious with which deity the cat is linked. On the approximately contemporary stela of the professional female mourner

58 A stela dedicated to the 'good and peaceful cat' by lady Hemetnetjer, from Deir el-Medina, *c.* 1270 BC. Turin, Museo Egizio.

Hemetnetjer, there are two 'hieroglyphic' cats facing each other, but in the text only the 'good and peaceful (female) cat' is asked to grant 'life, prosperity and health.' The gender of the animal suggests that this cat, shown twice for the sake of symmetry, is associated with a goddess, perhaps again Mut or, as we shall see later, Hathor Nebethetepet.

A stela of the draughtsman Nebre shows a swallow which, apparently, also received some kind of worship at Deir el-Medina, and 'the good (female) cat, enduring! enduring!'.

It is not always possible to decide whether the motif of a cat used on small objects should be regarded as purely decorative or whether religious connotations are present. Maybe it is wrong to ask such a question at all. Although their dating is not easy, amulets (statuettes) in the shape of cats, usually very small and made of Egyptian faience (glazed frit), were now common and probably linked with the cat's protective function in popular religion. The cat also occurred in the same role on finger-rings and earrings.

The cat on the base of a scarab-shaped amulet may be part of the 'trigram' of the god Amun. Amun of Thebes was the most important Egyptian deity from the beginning of the second millennium BC. His name was often inscribed on amulets, sometimes in a cryptographic form. A group of three hieroglyphs, consisting of the sun-disc + a cat + a basket, normally read *aten* + *miu* + *neb*, could convey the name of Amun by acrophony, the reading of the initial consonants only: *a* + *m* + *n* = *Amun*. Other combinations are more symbolic and not always easy to decipher, but that is one of the main difficulties accompanying the study of scarabs in general. For example, a cat may be combined with one or more lotus flowers, both symbols of regeneration.

59 A steatite scarab with the trigram of Amun, probably *c.*664–30 BC. British Museum.

Seals ('scaraboids,' so called because their shape initially was that of the scarab beetle), where a figure of the cat formed the part which the user handled, are also known. The name of the deity on the base, such as the Theban Amun-Ra, need not be directly linked to the cat.

The sistrum, or ceremonial rattle, was an instrument symbolically connected with the notion of regeneration and particularly associated with the goddess Hathor. It can be frequently seen in the hands of wives of high officials. Starting in the New Kingdom, one or more cats appeared quite often on Hathor-headed sistra associated with the goddess Nebethetepet. This was one of the many forms of the goddess Hathor and a companion of the creator-god Atum and sun-god Ra at Heliopolis. The goddess personified the creator-god's hand. In this way the Egyptian system of religious 'constellations' (groupings) overcame the difficulty posed by the absence of a female counterpart for the creator-god who, by definition, was alone. One of the most salient characteristics associated with the goddess Nebethetepet was sexual energy, and the original linking of the cat with this goddess was probably due to the animal's fertility and prodigious procreative powers.

Another object linked with Hathor and Nebethetepet was the *menat*, a multi-strand faience bead necklace with a solid faience counterpoise which sometimes carried representations of cats wearing such a necklace.

On stelae dedicated to Hathor and Nebethetepet by Kasa and his wife Bukhanef, of Deir el-Medina, there are two cats flanking the Hathor emblem consisting of a pillar or column with the head of the goddess shown in front view, as if it were its capital. Kasa and Bukhanef lived during the reign of Ramses II (1279–1213 BC). From at least as early as the ninth century BC, cats flanking such an emblem could be linked with the goddess Bastet but that need not have been the case in the New Kingdom. A temple-wall fragment from Bubastis, dated to the reign of Nectanebo II (360–342 BC), shows two cats with the Hathor emblem between them. The cats' heads are turned back towards it in a rather unusual posture; the context suggests an association with Hathor rather than Bastet.

The cat can also be found on large bowls decorated with Hathor-heads. One mentions Amenhotep III (1391–1353 BC) and was found, of all places, in the tomb of Akhenaten at Amarna; others are dated to the Ramesside period (1295–1069 BC). Hathor's face, enveloped by a massive wig, is either moulded in relief or painted, and flanked by vegetal motifs and seated cats.

Half way through the last century of the second millennium BC, Egypt entered a prolonged crisis during which rulers of several Delta cities vied for the control of the country. At the end of this period, which lasted for some 400 years, invasions of the Kushites from the south ('Nubian' Dynasty, Manetho's Twenty-fifth) and the Assyrians from the north-east compounded the com-

60 A fragment of an alabaster bowl decorated in high relief, with part of the Hathor-head and a cat. The bowl was inscribed with the names of Amenhotep III (1391–1353 BC) and Queen Tiy, but it was found in the tomb of Akhenaten (1353–1337 BC) at Amarna. The Brooklyn Museum.

plexity of the situation. It was resolved only when the prince of the city of Sais (modern Sa el-Hagar) in the western delta, Psamtek I (664–610 BC), was first recognized by the Assyrian king Ashurbanipal as a vassal ruler of Egypt, and then gained complete independence. The Ptolemaic historian Manetho says that one of the ruling families during this difficult period, his Twenty-second Dynasty (945–715 BC), originated in the city of Bubastis (a Graecised form of the ancient Egyptian Per-Bastet, 'House of the Goddess Bastet,' Tell Basta) in the south-eastern part of the Delta. The city of Bubastis goes back to the beginning of Egyptian history and building activities of all periods are well attested there. Bubastis did not now necessarily replace Memphis and Tanis (San el-Hagar, in the north-eastern Delta) as the country's administrative capital, but its importance was considerably enhanced and this led to extensive building activities in the local temple of the goddess Bastet by several kings, such as Osorkon I (924–889 BC) and Osorkon II (874–850 BC). The names of these kings suggest that their ancestors belonged to the Libyan ethnic element, which had always been very strongly represented among the inhabitants of the Delta.

The chief deity of the city was from the earliest times the goddess Bastet. Somewhat confusingly, her Graecised name was Bubastis, the same as the name of the locality, but this may have been due to misunderstanding on the part of Herodotus. Early representations of Bastet show a woman with the head of a lioness and a uraeus (serpent) on her forehead, holding a long sceptre in one hand, and an *ankh* ('life') sign in the other. In this form she already appears on stone vessels from Saqqara which mention King Hotepse-khemwy (*c*.2800 BC). Bastet was a goddess without a real name; hers means simply 'She of the City of Bast.' The lion god Mahes (Miysis or Mios in Greek) was regarded as her son. The goddess very soon began to be linked with other localities, in particular Memphis (perhaps through assimilation with another goddess represented as a lioness, Sekhmet, a companion of Ptah), Heliopolis where she was regarded as the daughter of the creator and sun god Atum, and Heracleopolis. She also became closely associated with several other goddesses, in particular Hathor, Mut, and Isis.

The name of Bastet often occurs in New Year's wishes found inscribed on various small items such as blue-glazed flasks which would have been New Year's gifts. The reason for this may have been that as a lioness goddess she was associated with the five epagomenal days of the Egyptian civil calendar, i.e. those which did not belong to any of the twelve months of thirty days each. These days were marked by religious festivals, but were also regarded as a dangerous period because of their unusual position within the year. The lioness goddesses, because of their bellicose character, would have been linked with these five days.

The Egyptians were used to thinking in terms of opposites, such as the day and the night, the Nile valley and the desert, Upper and Lower Egypt, the white and the red royal crowns, and many others. The goddesses Sekhmet and Bastet began to be paired as such opposites complementing each other as early as *c*.1850 BC. 'She rages like Sekhmet and she is friendly like Bastet' is how the goddess Hathor-Tefnut was described in *The Myth of the Eye of the Sun* in the temple at Philae some 1700 years later. Eventually they came to be thought of as aspects of the same goddess, one threatening and danger-ous, the other protective and peaceful.

We do not know precisely when the female cat started being regarded as a manifestation of Bastet but it is reasonably certain that it coincided with the rise to greater prominence of the city of Bubastis during the Twenty-second Dynasty (945–715 BC). The name of one of the kings of this dynasty was Pamiu, 'The Tomcat,' and he reigned between 773 and 767 BC. It may be that the link was mainly due to the physical similarity of the two animals, albeit on a different scale, and the comparable patterns of behaviour. The head of a lioness and that of a female cat are very difficult to distinguish in Egyptian art. The lion's main characteristics were strength and ferocity; the cat was its household counterpart, playful and affectionate. In the demotic *Instruction of Ankhsheshonq*, of the Ptolemaic period (after 332 BC) or even earlier, there is a rather more down-to-earth comparison of the two animals (translation by M. Lichtheim): 'When a man smells of myrrh, his wife is a cat before him. When a man is suffering, his wife is a lioness before him.'

Apart from her traditional representations as a lioness or a lioness-headed woman, the goddess Bastet could now be represented as a cat or cat-headed woman. We have seen that the image of the cat had been known in Egyptian religion for some thousand years earlier. We have noted the possibility that some of the goddesses regarded as the daughters of the sun-god and represented as lionesses may have been shown as cats already during the Ramesside period; the case remains to be argued fully and convincingly demonstrated. It seems that the image of a cat-headed woman may also have been known before. A goddess, who sometimes appears as an 'usherette' in scenes of the judgement of the deceased person known from one of the vignettes in the *Book of the Dead*, is usually nameless but may be Mafdet, the 'female panther' deity which combines the characteristics of big cats. In the 'mythological' papyrus of the songstress of the god Amun-Ra, king-of-the-gods, Dirpu, dated to *c.*1000 BC, such a goddess is shown bringing the deceased lady into the presence of Osiris, the ruler of the underworld. I have already remarked on the difficulties which we encounter when trying to distinguish between the heads of lions, cats, and probably also leopards and cheetahs. Here the body is that of a woman but the head is quite unmistakably that of a cat. It is, of course, quite clear that this cannot be Bastet. So it seems that iconographically the representations of Mafdet may have paved the way for Bastet.

Some statuettes portray both forms of Bastet, as a woman with the head of a lioness, accompanied by a small figure of a cat. A fragment of such a piece shows a seated goddess, almost certainly the warlike lioness-headed Sekhmet, with her feet resting on the backs of prostrate bound captives, while a cat is perched rather nonchalantly on their legs. Child-bearing and nurturing instincts figured prominently in the 'character' of Bastet and other goddesses who manifested themselves as lionesses; the king is often called their son. These were now combined with the cat's fertility, apparently boundless nocturnal love-life, and its old protective function, and so indicate the areas in which the goddess Bastet was popularly supplicated for help with human problems.

With the link between the two animals forged, it is easy to understand why extensive cat cemeteries appeared wherever the local goddess manifested

61 (*Left*) Bronze statuette of King Pamiu ('The Tomcat'), of the 22nd (Bubastite) Dynasty, offering jars of water. British Museum. 62 (*Right*) Glazed sandstone statuette of the lioness- (or cat-) headed Sekhmet/Bastet, with a bronze face, probably *c*.664–30 BC. British Museum.

herself as a lioness. Ultimately, they were all regarded as aspects of the same deity. An important cult of a lioness goddess was that of Pakhet (from *pakh*, 'to scratch,' literally 'She Who Scratches') at Istabl Antar (Speos Artemidos) near Beni Hasan in Middle Egypt. In the fourth century BC, a certain Pede-kem, buried at Tuna el-Gebel (the necropolis of Hermopolis), was a 'prophet of the living cat of the temple of Pakhet.' A large cemetery of such mummified temple cats was located in the vicinity of the temple.

Some of the goddesses to whom the cat was occasionally linked were not usually portrayed in the form of a lioness and so the connection must have been of a different, though not always obvious, kind. The most important among these was Neith, the goddess worshipped primarily at Sais (Sa el-Hagar) in the western delta.

A more widespread recognition of the cults with animals as their cult images, and the final stage in the cat's religious progress, started during the Late period (after 664 BC). The preceding four centuries witnessed enormous changes in the political life of the country, which must have been mirrored in the corresponding adjustments in the religious sphere. The increased popularity of local animal cults, such as that at Bubastis, may have been one of them. Nevertheless, the developments in the Late period could not have been an entirely spontaneous process but were at least partly a consequence of a deliberate policy of the kings of the Twenty-sixth (664–525 BC) and Thirtieth (380–343 BC) Dynasties, and then the early Ptolemies. These rulers introduced wide-ranging administrative reforms which actively encouraged the growth of the 'sacred animal industry' associated with temples and cemeteries so that the state became an active participant in the process. Not the smallest consideration would have been the fact that the numbers of people involved in these cults in various capacities (priestly, administrative, and menial) increased considerably. The state benefited fiscally from the sale of priestly offices, taxation of the institutions connected with the cults, and perhaps also from the donations made by pious worshippers.

The festival of the goddess Bastet at Bubastis became one of the largest and most popular in the country. These occasions usually included a ceremonial procession during which the image of the local deity was brought out and at least its portable shrine could be seen by ordinary people. In the fifth century BC, Herodotus described the large number of river boats on the way to the city, full of men and women making music, singing, and clapping their hands. He estimated that some 700,000 people attended such a festival of the goddess, whom he called Artemis. It is difficult to judge whether the inviting erotic gestures of the women pilgrims which he mentions were prompted by their pious zeal and served as a reference to the nature of the goddess, or were an expression of Chaucerian bawdy merriment. The festivities included large quantities of wine being consumed. Even wild animals associated with a deity could feel safe while festivities lasted; some 700 years earlier, Ramses IV (1153–1147 BC) claimed that he had not hunted lions during the festival of Bastet. Celebrations of Bastet were not confined to Bubastis but were also regular occasions at Esna and Thebes in Upper Egypt and in Memphis.

The growth in popularity of cults associated with animals accelerated during the Ptolemaic period. The earlier economic considerations still applied, but new dimensions may have been added as the result of altered political and religious circumstances. On the one hand, these cults could be seen as an expression of Egyptian nationalism and a means of uniting the Egyptian populace behind their traditional religious institutions at times when native beliefs and culture were forced on the defensive under pressure from foreign elements. On the other hand, they would have been a tangible proof of the new ruling group's wish to placate the religious feelings of the native population. It is interesting to note that a number of the devotees who dedicated votive items to Bastet had Greek names.

Bastet became a very common element of Ptolemaic personal names, and was surpassed in popularity only by the god Osiris. Names like Padibast/Tadibast (Greek Petobastis/Tetobastis) = '(S)he whom Bastet gave,' Bastetirdis = 'Bastet is she who gave him/her,' or Pashenubaste/Tashenubaste (Greek Psenobastis/Senobastis) = 'The Son/Daughter of Bastet,' suggest that the goddess was believed to have played a part in the child's conception or birth. Other names, such as Ankh-bastet = 'May Bastet live!' or Nakhtbasterau = 'Bastet is powerful against them,' are more general. It is possible that the attractive Pedemiu, 'He whom the cat gave,' is a ghost name, i.e. one which did not exist but was misread by Egyptologists. The hieroglyph of a cat may simply stand for the goddess Bastet, and the name be Padibast.

The popularity of animal cults and the zealous esteem in which they were held also had some adverse effects. In spite of its often terrifying imagery, ancient Egyptian religion could hardly be described as savage or militant. Indeed, while it played such an important part in everybody's life, a huge diversity of often contradictory views existed fairly amicably side by side. One of the hallmarks of ancient Egypt was a remarkable degree of ideological tolerance and common sense. Compliance and orthodoxy were, of course, expected, but religious persecution was unknown. For most of Egyptian history there were no attempts to spread the influence of a deity by violent means and no pogroms on those worshipping different gods. The pharaoh may have ascribed the motivation behind some of his acts, such as military campaigns abroad, to his attempts to please the gods, but his prime considerations were of a very practical nature. No edicts banning particular deities are known. Deep religious feelings were widespread, but exclusivist religious fanaticism seems to have been absent. There was only one attempt, under Akhenaten (1353–1337 BC), to alter the existing religious set-up in a radical fashion and to favour one god to the detriment of the others.

These circumstances, it seems, changed in the second half of the first millennium BC and the situation may have sometimes approached religious hysteria. Herodotus, who visited Egypt in the mid-fifth century BC, says that anybody who intentionally killed a sacred animal was put to death; an accidental killing was punished by whatever penalty the priests deemed appropriate. Diodorus confirms this statement and recounts an incident which he himself witnessed, probably in 59 BC during the reign of Ptolemy XI Auletes, in which a visiting member of a Roman delegation accidentally killed a cat. Neither the king's intervention nor delicate diplomatic considerations could save the man from being lynched by an angry mob. Even if a dead animal was spotted lying in the street people would avoid it for fear of being suspected of involvement in its death. Was something like this meant when the already mentioned sage Ankhsheshonq advised 'Do not laugh at a cat'?

The increase in the popularity of cats in late Egypt was reflected in the large numbers of bronze statuettes of these animals. The statuettes demonstrated the improved skills in bronze casting and the ability to produce on a large scale which characterized the progress of small arts in the first half of the first millennium BC. They may have been used in many ways. In a rather opportunist way, some of them may have held the cat remains in the hollow left after casting, and these were buried in cemeteries; small statuettes have also been found among the bandages of real animals. Others may have been fixed to small caskets which contained the cat's body. The majority of them were intended to be dedicated in a shrine.

The idea behind the gift of a statuette of a deity to the deity itself is interesting. It was a common custom in late Egypt to present a small monument to a temple, perhaps to commemorate a pilgrimage made on the occasion of a religious festival or as an expression of gratitude to the god for past favours or in expectation of such favours in the future. There were several types of these monuments, including images of the deity itself. The concept probably goes back to the time when it was only the king who provided temples with their cult images, such as statues, or renewed the existing ones. Gradually this royal prerogative was modified and became available to ordinary people. They were now allowed to leave a statuette representing the cult image in which the deity manifested itself (in this case a cat) on the temple's premises. These small items, usually only a few inches high, were probably bought in the local workshop and were kept in the temple for some time. When their accumulated numbers increased to such an extent that pressure for space made it rather awkward to retain them any longer, they were collected and buried in specially-prepared pits. There they may have been joined by various other items of temple furniture which may have got damaged or needed replacement but which had been associated with the structure for such a long time that it was not deemed proper to throw them away.

In the present state of our knowledge, it is very difficult to date the thousands of bronze statuettes of cats in museums and private collections with any precision. Most of them probably represent the cat of Bastet. It seems that the earliest among them date to about 900 BC (a statuette inscribed for one of the kings called Sesonchis) and others to the seventh and sixth

63 (*Right*) A bronze statuette of a cat, *c.*664–30 BC. As in almost all three-dimensional examples, its tail is neatly placed on the ground along the right side of the body. British Museum.

64 (*Far right*) A bronze statuette of a cat with gold earrings, probably *c.*664–30 BC. British Museum.

centuries BC (a statuette of a cat of Psamtek I, 664–610 BC), but the majority of them are Ptolemaic (after 332 BC). Inscribed statuettes are very exceptional. However, this may be because the pedestals to which many of them were originally attached, and which may have carried the name of the donor, were made of a different material, most probably wood, and these have now disappeared. When preserved, the pedestal may be in the shape of the *menat* counterpoise, with one end rounded and the other rectangular. The larger statuettes were made by hollow casting, the smaller are often solid cast. Many different types are known and anatomically most of them are remarkably accurate. The artist sometimes succeeded superbly in conveying the rather haughtily graceful dignity and aloofness of the animal, but there are also many examples of rather mediocre workmanship. The most common is the traditional 'hieroglyphic' image of a seated cat, albeit with the tail neatly lying on the ground along the paws. These vary in size from those which are only a few centimetres high to large life-size sculptures.

Details of the bronze statuettes, such as the eyes, ears, the pattern of the fur, and the animal's ornaments, may be picked out in gold. The cats often have their ears pierced for gold or silver earrings and some also wear a

65 (*Left*) A bronze statuette of a cat with its eyes, collar and details of the fur picked out in gold, probably *c*.664–30 BC. British Museum.

66 (*Below*) An amulet in the form of a small hollow-cast bronze figure of a cat and two kittens, with a ring for suspension, *c*.664–30 BC. British Museum.

nose-ring. On their head may be the sun-disc and uraeus (serpent), both deriving from the lioness-headed image of Bastet, and between their ears an image of the scarab beetle which indicated the cat's connection with the sun-god. A winged scarab may also appear on the chest. The eyes may be inlaid in rock crystal or similar opaque material. Round the neck there is occasionally a necklace of cowrie-shells or similar, often with a pendant, such as the *udjat*-eye of Horus, an 'aegis' consisting of a head of a deity with a broad collar, or a small figure of a deity. The fur is sometimes indicated by patterned incisions and several other techniques, as are the whiskers and the hairs in the ears. Exceptionally, much smaller kittens accompany an adult cat.

The cat in the Ramesside tomb of Penbuy and Kasa (TT 10, *c*.1250 BC) sports a collar-like necklace and earrings, and so we must accept that some domestic pets were made to look faintly ridiculous by wearing such ornaments, probably including a nose-ring. The scarab may reflect a natural marking of the fur. Some of the other adornments of these statuettes, however, imitate the features of the large temple images rather than living reality.

The cat's tail is invariably neatly placed on the ground along the right side of the animal, sometimes curled round the right forepaw. The reason for this

67 (*Above*) A large bronze statuette of a cat, *c.*664–30 BC, probably from Saqqara. British Museum.

68 (*Above, right*) A hollow-cast bronze statuette of a cat, *c.*664–30 BC, which is large enough to have been used to hold the remains of a real cat. It has an incised *udjat*-eye on its chest. British Museum.

69 (*Right*) A bronze statuette of a mother cat with three kittens being suckled, while a fourth is licking her nose, *c.*664–30 BC. British Museum.

70 (*Above*) A bronze statuette of 'housewife Bastet' holding a sistrum and aegis, with four kittens, *c*.664–30 BC. British Museum.

71 (*Above, right*) A bronze hollow-cast statuette of 'housewife Bastet' wearing a patterned dress and carrying a sistrum and aegis, accompanied by kittens, *c*.664–30 BC. British Museum.

72 (*Right*) A bronze statuette of the household god Bes, wearing a feathered crown, between two cats, *c*.664–30 BC. British Museum.

73 (*Right*) A bronze statuette of 'housewife Bastet,' with her eyes highlighted in gold, probably c.664–30 BC. British Museum.

74 (*Far right*) A bronze statuette of 'housewife Bastet' wearing a contemporary Hellenistic (though not necessarily un-Egyptian) dress, 1st century AD. British Museum.

lies in the conventions of Egyptian two-dimensional art and script in which animals looked to their right. The tail would have been almost completely obscured if it had been placed along the other side of the body, and this would not have been artistically acceptable.

Cats shown in other positions are also known. Those lying down with their kittens are well attested, but there are also standing, walking, crouching or sleeping animals. Groups of several adult cats also occur.

Some statuettes may show the cat in the company of a deity other than Bastet, such as Nefertem (originally regarded as the son of the goddess Sekhmet at Memphis and then similarly linked with Bastet), Osiris, or the dwarf house-god Bes. The cat may be supporting it, being carried on its shoulders, or just sitting at its feet. A worshipper may sometimes kneel in adoration in front of a cat.

Another common type of a bronze statuette shows Bastet as a cat-headed goddess dressed in a tightly-fitting patterned ankle-length dress (less usually one which reveals the knees), holding a sistrum in one hand and the aegis of the lioness-headed Sekhmet, her alter ego, in the other. She sometimes also holds a small figure of the god Nefertem. It has been suggested that the patterned or sometimes striped gown imitates the tabby coat of the Egyptian cat, and while this is a most attractive theory, it would be difficult to prove it. These statuettes at first appear fairly uniform but, in fact, they display a large variety of details. The ears may be pierced for earrings. In some statuettes, the feline characteristics are confined to the head of the deity while others show the cat's hind paws and a tail showing beneath the dress. Sometimes the goddess is wearing a non-Egyptian free-flowing robe, such as we see in Hellenistic statues of the goddess Isis. A round basket may be shown dangling from one of her elbows. This may have been intended for carrying kittens, but a definite proof of this theory is lacking. Small figures of cats sometimes accompany her, or the house-dwarf Bes may stand rather awkwardly next to her feet. These are charming statuettes for which some Egyptologists have coined the phrase 'housewife Bastet' because one cannot help comparing them to ordinary housewives on the way to do their shopping in the local supermarket.

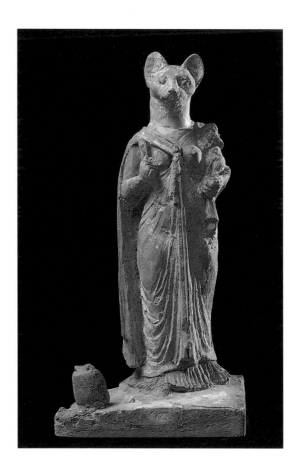

75 A variant of the cat-headed 'housewife Bastet' statuettes, this time with the goddess carrying a child and wearing a long flowing robe. Painted and gilded limestone, 1st century AD. Hildesheim, Pelizaeus-Museum.

Cat statuettes of all types were also made in other materials, such as different kinds of stone (limestone, lapis lazuli, breccia, agate, quartz, haematite, etc.), faience, glass, pottery or wood. Smaller sculptures, including some bronze pieces, have a large ring in the shoulder area, presumably to allow them to be attached to garments or to be part of personal jewellery such as necklaces. These were then used as amulets and worn for protection.

Inscriptions on cat statuettes are usually limited to the names of the deity and the donor and a simple wish, e.g. 'Twice. May Great Bastet, the Mistress of Bubastis, give life to Horemheb, for ever!' or 'May Bastet, Mistress of Ankh-tawy (= Memphis), make life and protection!'

The figure of a 'cat on a column' is found on bronze terminals which imitate either a papyrus umbel or a lotus flower and are reminiscent of architectural column-capitals, hence the term. The lotus, as a symbol of regeneration, would have been particularly appropriate, but the shape of the column is often rather ambiguous. Originally, I presume, the objects were attached to staves or sticks. These would have been more than ordinary walking sticks

76 (*Right*) A bronze sistrum with a recumbent cat and two kittens on top of the arch, and another cat seated below, 1st century AD. British Museum.

77 (*Far right*) A cat seated at the base of the arch of a bronze Hathor-headed sistrum, c.332–30 BC. British Museum.

78 (*Above*) A faience statuette of cat-headed Bastet holding an *udjat*-eye, *c*.664–30 BC. British Museum.

79 (*Above, right*) A small faience statuette-amulet of cat-headed Bastet, *c*.664–30 BC. British Museum.

80 (*Right*) A small faience quadriform (representing four figures) amulet of the goddess Bastet, probably from Abydos, *c*.664–30 BC. British Museum.

81 (*Above*) A faience amulet in the form of a spotted (tabby) cat, 1st century AD. British Museum.

82 (*Above, right*) A small faience amulet with a suspension ring, representing a cat and kittens, *c.*664–30 BC. British Museum.

83 (*Right*) A blue faience amulet with a suspension ring, a cat and a kitten, *c.*664–30 BC. British Museum.

84 (*Below, left*) A faience amulet, a cat turning its head, perhaps from Memphis, 1st century AD. British Museum.

85 (*Below, right*) A faience amulet showing two cats seated on top of a papyrus column, *c.*664–30 BC. British Museum.

86 A bronze handle, probably from a vessel or a furniture fitting, with a seated cat, c.664–30 BC. British Museum.

and may have designated the holder's office or priestly function. Another possibility is that they formed decorative finials of furniture such as palanquins or litters. The cat is usually seated or crouching and may be accompanied by a kitten. The motif was adopted in the manufacture of faience amulets where the cat has the usual ring for suspension in the shoulder area.

We have already seen that shortly before the beginning of the New Kingdom (c.1540 BC) the cat appeared on ladies' personal jewellery such as bracelets, where its religious protective role may have been combined with purely aesthetic considerations. Small figures of cats continued to be used throughout Egyptian history on faience finger-rings and, in particular, as elements of necklaces in various materials. The cat may also be found on items of, apparently, 'daily life,' such as vase-handles and skewers or large pins.

Sometimes the motif of a cat is, quite frankly, perplexing. How does one explain the decoration of a faience pectoral (a plaque in the shape of a small naos which was placed on the breast of a human mummy) which consists of a large fish, with another small fish and a cat below? That this was not a mere whim of the craftsman goes without saying, but what was the symbolism behind it?

Sistra (rattles) with the figures of cats were now often linked with the goddess Bastet by their inscriptions.

With the loss of Egyptian independence to Rome in 30 BC the more formal aspects of Egyptian religion started losing ground and the process accelerated when Christianity reached the country. The traditional beliefs of ordinary people would have survived longer and when in the fourth to fifth centuries AD Shenute, the head of the White Monastery at Sohag in Middle Egypt, waged war on pagans and their abominable religious practices, these must have been adherents of the old Egyptian deities. Theirs was a losing fight and with the demise of their beliefs the cat also lost its divinity and returned to its original role of a domestic animal and pet. In Egypt, at least, it did not fare too badly, although the contents of some of the Greek papyri with magical texts from Egypt, probably dating to the fourth century AD, ominously include spells to be recited while drowning a cat. Elsewhere it was a different story.

87 A bronze statuette of a cat and four kittens (one licking its mother's nose, two being suckled, and the fourth playing with the cat's hind paw), c.664–30 BC. British Museum.

Pride goes before a fall
The story cats

The sources which are available to us for the study of ancient Egypt chiefly inform us about the lives of the wealthy and privileged members of Egyptian society. These were the people who were buried in large decorated tombs, had their statues set up in temples, and left autobiographical texts. We know considerably less about those who built and decorated the tombs, manufactured the statues and carved the inscriptions. The largest section of the Egyptian population were peasants, whom we only encounter as anonymous background figures in reliefs and paintings or as faceless names in administrative documents. When, therefore, we talk about arts and religion we must not forget that Egypt was a multifaceted and multilayered society and that the differences between the 'official' (reflected in monuments and other records) and the 'unofficial' (left unrecorded) must have been enormous.

One of the few exceptions to the usual paucity of information concerning the Egyptian 'working classes' is the community of artisans who were employed in the construction and decoration of royal tombs of the pharaohs of the New Kingdom (1540–1069 BC). Their settlement was at Deir el-Medina, in the desert on the west bank of the Nile at Thebes, and their workplace was the Valley of the Kings. These stonemasons, sculptors, and painters were very skilled workmen and employees of the state. They were certainly no paupers, but must have been well off by contemporary standards. The level of literacy among these people was unusually high and the number of documents concerning all aspects of their lives which have survived is very large. Some of these were written in ink on papyri, the most popular writing material, made from the pith of the *Cyperus papyrus L.* reed. More casual notes and jottings were made on ostraca (from the Greek *ostrakon*, 'potsherd'), flakes of smooth white limestone which were much cheaper and of which there was an inexhaustible supply in the area. The script used for writing on ostraca was the cursive 'hieratic' (the relationship between the hieratic script and the hieroglyphs, which we can see on temple and tomb walls, can be compared to that of our handwriting and print). The majority of the papyri and ostraca found in the village of Deir el-Medina or in the Valley of the Kings date to the Ramesside period, *c.*1295–1069 BC, which represented the peak in the fortunes of the settlement.

On some of the ostraca there are very quickly but skilfully sketched representations which may suggest that these small objects were used as informal jotting pads. We find there details of large scenes which we know from tomb walls and stelae and even some which are new, either because the idea was abandoned or because the more accomplished version has not survived. Some, particularly sketches of animals, appear to have been made purely for pleasure. The cat occurs several times. One ostracon shows it carrying a mouse or rat in its mouth. Another depicts a man in front of a large cat. This is a statue rather than a live animal, and it is interesting to see how the artist solved the problem of the disproportionate sizes of the two figures. The cat is placed on a pedestal and its height seems further increased by a large sun-shade behind it. On another ostracon, there is a woman kneeling in front of a cat, an artistic solution which is even more effective. A young boy, his arm raised, faces a large mean-looking cat, as if trying to chase it away or hit it with whatever he may be holding in his hand.

Other ostraca are of a rather special kind. Many depict scenes involving animals, among which cats are well represented. One shows a tabby cat, upright on its hind paws, with a stick in one front paw while steadying a pole with a jar and a basket slung over its shoulder with the other. Ducks walk in two orderly rows in front of their duckherd, a cat. On another ostracon there is a lady mouse or rat, dressed up in a fine pleated garment, seated on a folding stool the legs of which imitate duck necks and heads. It holds a lotus flower rather delicately in one 'hand' while enjoying a drink through a long

88 A painted ostracon, perhaps from Deir el-Medina and dated to c.1150 BC. A cat, holding a fan and a napkin, presents a roasted goose to a seated rat. The Brooklyn Museum.

drinking tube from a large wine-jar. Two adult cats are in attendance – one doing up the rat's hair, the other, accompanied by a kitten, looking after the supply of wine. Several variants of the scene are known. One shows a rat smelling a lotus flower, its hind 'feet' resting on a small mat, and a cat in attendance in front of it. In another, a cat acting as a servant girl holds a fan and a hand-cloth while presenting a seated cat with a roasted goose. Yet another scene shows a rat witnessing the punishment of a young offender which is being meted out with a large stick by a cat, while on another ostracon the roles of the punishing and the punished are reversed. Other animals, too, appear in most unlikely situations. The fox is shown playing the double oboe to a dancing goat, making music as a member of a troupe of musicians, or brewing beer with an antelope as its helper. Several foxes can be seen fanning a lady mouse, bringing her flowers and serenading her. Monkeys in the role of gardeners are watering a vegetable plot, playing the double oboe for a male dancer, or driving a chariot. A mouse can also be shown as a chariot driver or a juggler. In a breathtakingly sacrilegious scene, a mouse is carried in a portable shrine by jackals as though it were a deity, with a monkey spreading its paws behind it in a gesture of protection. On another ostracon, a dog may be seen walking up the staircase leading to a building, perhaps a temple.

The situations depicted are strange and appear to have nothing to do with

89 The nightmare of a cat tormentor? An ostracon, probably from Deir el-Medina and dated to *c*.1150 BC, with a cat chastising a young offender. Chicago, Oriental Institute.

90 A tabby cat, with a basket with provisions slung on a pole, herding a flock of geese. An ostracon from Deir el-Medina, *c.*1150 BC. Cairo, Egyptian Museum.

the decoration of the tombs and the formal images of Egyptian art. Or have they? The figure of a herdsman carrying a water jar and a basket with provisions on a pole over the shoulder was a motif with which every tomb-artist would have been familiar. Rather formal representations of seated ladies indulging at banquets or attended by their housemaids must have been so common that every tomb draughtsman must have been heartily sick of them. Brewers, gardeners, and musicians were represented in tombs. Occasions during which a portable shrine with a divine image was carried in procession can be seen on tomb as well as temple walls. Is it not likely, then that these ostraca simply stand for the one thing which no society, however pious or authoritarian, can ever prevent, namely humour?

Literary sources suggest that in spite of, or may be because of, the seemingly crushing formality pervading Egyptian society there was a strong undercurrent of irreverence and healthy scepticism among its inhabitants. In this respect, modern Egypt is remarkably similar. The scenes on the ostraca combine two things. The first is a refreshingly cynical view concerning the relationship between the real world and tomb art. The other is an acute observation of the character of various animals, in particular cats – we have already seen that there are more cats in the paintings in Deir el-Medina tombs than anywhere else in Egypt – combined with a rather shrewd comparison with people. The relative sizes of the protagonists do not correspond to reality and this suggests that rather than animal species they represent types which can be met in the animal world as well as among people. Cats are natural comics but their haughtily independent and proud demeanour makes them an inherent butt for humour. There is nothing an ordinary man of today likes better than when a public figure is brought down as the result of his or her indiscreet or arrogant behaviour. It seems that the ancient Egyptians were not much different. What is reflected in these ostraca is irreverent, at times slightly vulgar, but probably not much more than that. It is unlikely that the sketches were illustrations of fables with a moral content. Nor do they seem to have been intended to act as a satire containing veiled criticism aimed at the more privileged groups of Egyptian society.

I would like to imagine a group of workmen sitting in the shade, just inside the entrance to one of the royal tombs, taking a brief rest from their work in a dark and dusty environment, perhaps annoyed by the behaviour of their superior or angry at the delay in their payment. One of them, who has spent the whole morning drawing scenes which his colleagues will then complete in colour or carve into the surface of the tomb wall, has picked up a limestone fragment and starts, almost absent-mindedly, sketching on it. His colleagues watch his effort with amusement but also some professional interest and pass

91 A sketch of a cat with long ears, on an ostracon, *c.*1250 BC. Compare the cats on the stela of Hemetnetjer, fig.58. Hildesheim, Pelizaeus-Museum.

the finished ostracon from hand to hand, perhaps making disparaging remarks or jokingly adding a slightly coarse detail here and there. There are times when one feels like a little mouse pursued by the mighty cats of this world, and it is nice to think that the situation might be turned upside down. These people must have known the feeling and must have been just as prone to daydreaming as we are, and so they created a topsy-turvy world which existed only in their imagination.

The scenes on the ostraca were not necessarily always invented on the spur of the moment but became a genre which would have been improvised and repeated on many occasions. Nevertheless, the point which most of them make seems sufficiently clear and they do not require a story or a fable to explain them or justify their existence.

A few of the ostraca are different and it appears that these do, indeed, illustrate episodes from stories. One of them shows a monkey seated in front of a large cat (almost certainly not *Felis silvestris libyca*), with a bird, perhaps a vulture, nesting on eggs above. These animals appear in *The Myth of the Eye of the Sun*, recorded in demotic on three papyri dated to the second century AD, and also known from a Greek version. This is, of course, much later than the ostraca but there is some evidence to show that the theme was known already in the New Kingdom (1540–1069 BC). Indeed, its predecessor may be *The Book of the Divine Cow*, in which the goddess Hathor turns into

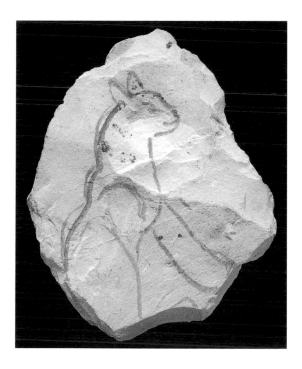

92 A sketch of a cat, perhaps a household animal, on an ostracon, probably *c.*1300–1100 BC. Cambridge, Fitzwilliam Museum.

the terrifying goddess Sekhmet and punishes those who plotted against her father Ra. Only getting her drunk prevents her from bringing about the destruction of the whole of humankind. Scarabs which show a cat in front of a wine jar may refer to this story and show the pacified aspect of the goddess.

The Myth of the Eye of the Sun concerns Tefnut, the daughter of the sun-god Ra whose eye she personifies. The beginning of the text is lost but presumably described how the father and his daughter quarrelled and how Tefnut in anger went to live abroad, in the south, in various animal forms, including that of a wild 'Nubian cat.' After some time the god Ra became lonely and wished to see his daughter again. So he sent the god Thoth, in the form of a monkey or a baboon, as his ambassador to plead with Tefnut. The goddess displays the two contradictory characteristics which we have seen embodied in Bastet, a raging lioness and a peaceful cat. When Thoth meets her, she is at her most threatening and he needs all his diplomatic skills to save his life. He entertains the goddess by telling her various stories, including one about a mother vulture and mother cat and their uneasy relationship. Eventually he succeeds in persuading her to return to Egypt, pacified and benign, and be reunited with her father at Memphis. The myth is also known from hiero-glyphic texts found in several temples of the Greco-Roman period, in particular Philae, but also at Kom Ombo, Esna, Edfu, Dendera, and some Nubian temples. The goddess is described by a variety of names, such as Sekhmet, Tefnut, Hathor, or 'Eye of the god Ra'. As daughters of the sun-god, these goddesses in their anger represented the cruel and dangerous aspects of the sun which had to be appeased and pacified.

Three fragmentary Ramesside (*c.*1295–1069 BC) papyri contain a whole

93 A cat as a female servant fanning a seated lady rat who holds a lotus flower to her nose. An ostracon, probably from Deir el-Medina, dated to *c.*1150 BC. Brussels, Musées Royaux d'Art et d'Histoire.

Two scenes reconstructed from a satirical papyrus probably from Deir el-Medina, *c.*1250–1100 BC, Turin, Museo Egizio. 94 (*Top*) Mice besieging a fortress defended by cats. 95 A cat savaged by a goose, another acting as a gooseherd and other scenes.

series of illustrations comparable to those on the ostraca, and probably also come from Deir el-Medina. One of them, in the Museo Egizio in Turin, is better known for its 'erotic' part. This is the closest we get to pornography in a culture which, we are sometimes told, hardly knew sex, only 'fertility.' It must be admitted that, when compared, the activities of animals are more amusing though not necessarily so imaginative as those of their human counterparts. There is a remarkable sequence of scenes which starts with mice besieging a fort defended by a garrison of cats. Here the audacious artist sailed perilously close to danger. A mouse in a dog-drawn chariot, discharging its arrows, cannot fail to remind one of King Ramses triumphant in the battle scenes in Egyptian temples, such as the pylon of the Luxor temple. This monumental entrance to the temple was accessible to the public and everybody would have known it intimately. The king mouse is preceded by infantrymice with spears, shields and bows, one of them climbing a siege ladder. Their opponents include a defiant cat archer; the other cats have either been slain or are begging for mercy. If one forgets that the protagonists are mice and cats this scene could illustrate one of the victorious Ramesside campaigns into Palestine or Syria. Then there is a duel between a cat and a mouse in which the weapons are curved cudgels. The final episode shows the chief of the cats surrendering to the mice. Tales about wars between cats and mice,

96 A fragment of a satirical papyrus of *c*. 1150 BC, showing a cat herding a flock of geese and a fox looking after a herd of goats while playing the double oboe. British Museum.

in which the traditional patterns of animal behaviour are reversed, have been recorded in various parts of the Near East and it is tempting to derive them from an ancient Egyptian prototype. The theme, however, is not known from Egyptian literature and so it is not certain whether these drawings should be regarded as illustrations of such a hypothetical story or mere elaboration of an idea which might appear independently anywhere.

The next strip on the Turin papyrus shows chain gangs of various animal miscreants being escorted by another animal. They include a cat with its front paws in a wooden *sheyba*, a device for immobilizing the hands of prisoners or captives, known from tomb and temple reliefs. There is a scene in an animal court presided over by an ass as a judge. Several apparently isolated scenes include a remarkable orchestra which includes a donkey as a harpist, a lion as a lyre-player, a crocodile as a lutenist, and a monkey playing the double oboe. Such a cartoon would be dynamite in the cultural world of today and one wonders how well such a 'review' was received three thousand years ago by the artists who may have felt themselves caricatured. The duckherd scene is also included and is enriched by an episode showing a cat, lying on its back, being savaged by a goose. Another cat is either trying to cool the combatants' tempers by throwing a jar of water over them or is attempting to revive the flagging fighting spirit of its comrade. This could be the continuation of the tense confrontation under a chair shown in the Deir el-Medina tomb of Penbuy and Kasa, which the author of the drawing on the papyrus may have known. Next to it, a bird needs a ladder to climb a tree while a hippopotamus is hopping nimbly in its branches picking figs into a basket.

A similar papyrus in the Egyptian Museum in Cairo shows cats as attendants

97 The top part of a faience figurine of the dwarf god Bes, with the scene of a cat and three geese on his crown, c.664–30 BC. Musée du Louvre.

98 Detail of the cat as gooseherd, from the satirical papyrus in the British Museum.

99 A procession of cats as household servants attending to a seated lady mouse or rat. Note the cat carrying a baby mouse in a sling. A satirical papyrus dating to c.1150 BC. Cairo, Egyptian Museum.

of a seated lady mouse, including one doing up her large wig, another plying her with drink, a cat nurse carrying a baby mouse in a sling, and another holding a large fan. The third such papyrus is a fragment in the British Museum. It shows a cat as a duckherd, and two others as servants of a lady mouse. There is also a remarkable scene of a lion and a gazelle playing *senet*, a board game vaguely reminiscent of our draughts. There may be a hint of irreverence even here if one recalls the scenes in the temple at Medinet Habu in which Ramses III (1184–1153 BC) is playing games with his harem ladies.

Occasional examples of the theme of animals behaving like people are attested throughout the rest of Egyptian history, albeit infrequently. Sometimes they appear in surprising contexts which are difficult to explain. A faience piece, which apparently formed the upper part of a figurine of the dwarf house-god and ladies' companion Bes, shows a scene with a cat herding three large geese, depicted on the dwarf's crown, as if on a fool's-cap. Very unusual reliefs from the temple at Medamud, north of Luxor, dating to *c.*mid-seventh century BC, show a feast in honour of a mouse, with a cat as a house servant and a crocodile playing the lute, and jackals as cooks. A pottery relief of the first or second century AD shows a cat and a mouse engaged in a fistfight refereed by an eagle. The last known examples occur in the art of the Egyptian Christians, the Copts. A fresco from the monastery of Apa Apollo in Bawit, in Middle Egypt, dating to the seventh or eighth century AD, shows what looks like negotiations between a cat (perhaps called 'cat of Buto') and a delegation of mice.

None of the later examples, however, can compare with the variety and number of themes known from Deir el-Medina, nor with the witty characterization and effortless technique of the Ramesside artists.

100 A cat and a mouse engaged in a boxing match supervised by an eagle, on a moulded pottery relief of the 1st or 2nd century AD. Copenhagen, Ny Carlsberg Glyptotek.

Buried with full honours
The mummified cats

The earliest evidence for the cat in Egypt comes from a grave to which, it seems, the animal accompanied its master. There is nothing to show whether the two died together or whether the animal was hastened to its death so that the two would not be separated. Be that as it may, the idea that animals may be buried just like human beings, or in their company, appeared well before the beginning of the Egyptian historic period and such burials are known from all times. It is certain that some of the animals regarded as manifestations of deities, such as the Apis-bull associated with the god Ptah at Memphis, or the Mnevis-bull of the sun-god Ra (or Atum) of On (Heliopolis), were buried in a simple fashion from the earliest times. For the first 1500 years of Egyptian history these were, however, exceptional cases.

A decisive change in the official attitudes towards cults in which a live animal was regarded as the deity's manifestation took place after 1400 BC, during the reign of Amenhotep III (1391–1353 BC). The king now began to take an active interest in them, particularly in the burial arrangements which had to be made after the animal's death. Some of the ideas about humans' life after death were also applied to these animals so that their tombs increased in size and rudimentary mummification procedures, depending on the species, were used. At Saqqara, the main necropolis of ancient Memphis south-west of modern Cairo, the earliest large tombs of the Apis-bulls date from this period. This development may have been one of the signs warning of an approaching far-reaching ideological crisis which was to shatter the cosy world of Egyptian religion during the reign of the king's son and successor, Akhenaten (1353–1347 BC). Nevertheless, one wonders whether at least some degree of personal motivation and general interest in animals may have played a part in it as well. It would have been the duty of the high priest of Ptah to supervise the burial of the Apis-bull, who had his living quarters in Ptah's temple at Memphis. We know that during the reign of Amenhotep III this office was held by his eldest son and heir designate, Prince Djehutymose, who would have succeeded his father if he had not predeceased him. As it happened, Amenhotep III was followed by his son of the same name, the future Akhenaten, whose views on Egyptian religion were of a different, much more radical and iconoclastic kind.

A small limestone sarcophagus made for a cat and bearing the titles and

name of the same Prince Djehutymose was found at Memphis. It is rectangular, with a vaulted lid, and its incised inscriptions and representations imitate
in an almost disturbing fashion scenes on human funerary monuments. The
texts include declarations of the goddesses Isis and Nephthys about the protection which they promise to give to the cat Tamyt. This was the name of
the animal but did not amount to much more than 'The Female Cat.' The
corners of the sarcophagus bear the names of the four 'Sons of Horus,' Hapy,
Qebhsenuef, Duamutef, and Imsety, who acted the protectors of the body.
The cat is 'Osirified', i.e. identified with the god Osiris, the ruler of the
underworld, in the same way as all people were after death. On the lid she
addresses the sky goddess Nut and wishes to become an 'imperishable star,'
a reference to the ancient belief that a deceased person (at first perhaps only
the king) ascended into the sky and became one of the circumpolar stars.
The text guarantees that 'the limbs of Tamyt, one true of voice before the
great god, shall not be weary.' The cat is shown in her 'hieroglyphic' image
in front of a table with offerings which include a duck and, rather illogically
in her case, some vegetables. She wears a *menat* necklace with a decorative
counterpoise. Behind the animal, there is a standing cat mummy, with the
body tightly wrapped up in bandages and topped with a cat-headed mask.
This suggests that, at least in some cases, cats were mummified already around
1350 BC, but it must be stressed that there is nothing to show that this
particular animal was in any way connected with a deity. Everything points to
her being a beloved pet. It is, of course, possible that when we credit Prince
Djehutymose with special affection for animals we are, in a rather sentimental
but mistaken way, trying to link a general trend in Egyptian religion with a
personal characteristic. The connection may be rather flimsy and there are
other examples of myths in Egyptology created in modern times.

Mummification, or the art of preservation of the dead in a nearly life-like
form, is such an unusual concept that it holds morbid fascination for many
people. The word for mummies derives from the Arabic *mumiya*, 'wax,' 'bitumen,' perhaps because of their blackened appearance, although Dead Sea
bitumen has been identified in some late specimens. The over-emphasis
placed on this aspect of Egyptian culture by non-specialists is more often
than not detrimental to the serious study of ancient Egypt and has resulted
in the less than favourable popular image of Egyptologists, demonstrated by
many novels and films.

It is true that the majority of monuments which have survived from ancient
Egypt and which Egyptologists study, and non-specialists admire, are funerary and come from tombs. Many others are connected with the worship of
deities and originate in temples. Only very few items in museum collections
were found in the excavations of towns and villages and had been used by

ordinary people in everyday life. There are many reasons for this, in particular the chances of preservation which favour tombs made at the edge of the desert rather than houses situated in the densely-populated Nile valley and the delta. Stone-built tombs and temples were also able to withstand the ravages of time infinitely better than mud-brick houses. Some of the best and most loved Egyptian artistic creations, such as statues and scenes carved in relief into stone, were specially made for tombs and temples and simply would not have existed without them. Religion and belief in life after death formed an essential part of everyday existence in ancient Egypt and cannot be separated from its other aspects. The study of this type of evidence significantly contributes to our knowledge of ancient Egyptian culture but, unless we are careful, we may obtain a rather biased and distorted image.

A human being could manifest itself in several 'modes of existence,' as a body, but also immaterially as *ka*, *ba*, or a name, although none of these must be seen purely mechanically as the person's 'components.' Death was not the end but, provided certain conditions were fulfilled, the threshold to a different form of life. The various 'modes of existence' were mutually dependent on each other so that preservation of the body was an essential condition for continued life after death.

The traditional way of explaining the origins of mummification is almost certainly rather simplistic but basically correct. During the predynastic period bodies of the dead were interred in ordinary graves dug at the edge of the

101 The stone sarcophagus of Tamyt, the cat of Prince Djehutymose, *c.*1350 BC, found at Memphis. Cairo, Egyptian Museum.

desert, and in the dry sand and hot climate they were often preserved by natural means. With the introduction of coffins and the enlargement and elaboration of tombs these conditions changed and so it was necessary to try and achieve by artificial means what previously nature had accomplished unaided. The methods of mummification continued to develop throughout Egyptian history and there was a considerable diversity according to the status and means of the deceased. Two stages of the process were essential for its success: evisceration, i.e. the removal of the inner organs (practised from about 2500 BC), and dehydration of the body by natron (a naturally-occurring dehydrating agent, a mixture of sodium carbonate and bicarbonate, with which the body was covered and packed during the period set aside for mummification). Various exotic materials were also used but their contribution to the successful outcome of the operation was limited. When the treatment of the body had been completed, it was wrapped up in bandages, often very elaborate, and put into one or more coffins and sarcophagi. These were placed in the tomb's burial chamber which was then closed and sealed.

Large animal cemeteries were a feature of the first millennium BC. They became more common towards the end of the Late period, from c.400 BC and after, but the majority of them date to the Ptolemaic period (332–30 BC), therefore they are later than pharaonic civilization proper. The vast increase in the quantities of animals which now began to be mummified, or at least buried, was due to the large numbers kept within temple precincts and to an extension of the concept of 'manifestation of the god' to some household animals. Almost the whole animal world is represented among these mummies: cattle, lions, crocodiles, rams, dogs, cats, baboons, ichneumons, ibises, falcons, shrewmice, snakes, fish, and others.

In the mid-fifth century BC, Herodotus wrote that when a cat died, the inhabitants of the house shaved their eyebrows as a sign of mourning; dead cats were, according to him, taken to the city of Bubastis (Tell Basta) where they were embalmed and buried. The cat cemeteries in the vicinity of the temple of the goddess Bastet at Bubastis may, indeed, have been among the earliest large animal necropoli and date from c.900 BC. Several other sites have yielded large quantities of mummified cats. The location of cat cemeteries was not accidental. At Bubastis, Saqqara and Istabl Antar they were situated close to the temples of the local deities Bastet, Sekhmet/Bastet and Pakhet. Most of the cats came from catteries attached to these temples and had been cared for by the personnel belonging to these institutions.

The cat cemetery at Tell Basta, in the south-eastern delta, was pillaged and almost completely destroyed in the second half of the nineteenth century, before it could be investigated by archaeologists. E. Naville, who excavated there on behalf of the Egypt Exploration Fund in the late 1880s, described dramatically the 'heaps of white bones of cats' littering the site, mixed with bronze statuettes and cat masks. He believed that the presence of furnaces indicated that the animals were not mummified but cremated, and Egyptologists have most recently tried to defend this view and support it by the already quoted remarks of Herodotus concerning house fires. Nevertheless, I think that this proposition is very unlikely; the whole concept of cremation would contradict all we know about Egyptian ideas concerning life after death of people as well as animals.

At Saqqara, south-west of Cairo, mummified cats were found close to the Bubastieion, the precinct of the goddess Bastet. Its beginnings may date to the Late period, perhaps to King Ahmose (570–526 BC), but it was especially important during the Ptolemaic period (332–30 BC). This was one of several temple structures situated at the eastern edge of the pyramid plateau, near the beginning of the approach to the main feature of the local sacred animal necropolis, the Serapeum with the tombs and chapels of the Apis-bulls. The connection of this area with the goddess Bastet may go as far back as the New Kingdom (1540–1069 BC), although no temple remains of such an early date have yet been located. The location of the temple cattery has not been

102 (*Right*) The most common type of cat mummy, with a conical body and the head modelled in linen and plaster, probably *c*.332–30 BC. British Museum.

103 (*Far right*) A cat mummy displaying an elaborate meander-pattern of bandaging. From Abydos, *c*.332–30 BC. British Museum.

established so far but it would have been in one of the buildings adjacent to the temple. New-Kingdom rock-cut tombs (locally known as *abwab el-qutat*, 'cat galleries') in a *wadi* (valley) nearby were used as depositories for cat burials.

The cemeteries with extensive deposits of mummified cats at Istabl Antar (Speos Artemidos), south of Beni Hasan in Middle Egypt, have been subjected to large-scale pillaging and illicit excavating but they have never been scientifically examined. They are situated close to the mouth of a *wadi* near the rock-cut temple of the goddess Pakhet, commissioned by Queen Hatshepsut around 1470 BC. Pakhet is first attested in the Middle Kingdom (2040–1648 BC) but a sanctuary of this period has not yet been located.

From Thebes, we know about 'the resting-place of the cats' mentioned in a demotic papyrus of the mid-second century BC, and contemporary documents in Greek refer to the privileges enjoyed by people connected with cat cemeteries. Mummified cats were found at Dra Abu 'l-Naga, on the west bank of the Nile.

During the Ptolemaic period cats would have been buried in animal cemeteries in all parts of Egypt, and cat burials or cat mummies have been also reported from near Tanis in the delta, Giza, Akhmim, Abydos, Dendera, the Dakhla Oasis, and several other places. It is impossible to estimate the numbers of animals involved with any accuracy but hundreds of thousands,

104 An unusually fine bronze cat mask with meticulously indicated whiskers and hairs. From Bubastis, *c.*664–30 BC. British Museum.

possibly millions, are indicated. An idea may be gleaned from the example of a single shipment of cat remains, weighing about nineteen tons and thought to have contained some 180,000 mummified cats, which was sent to England to be processed to make fertilizer towards the end of the last century.

Diodorus described the mummification of sacred animals in the first century BC although, like many other writers, he did not quite appreciate the main principles of the technique. According to him, the body was wrapped up in fine linen and treated with cedar oil and spices before being deposited in the tomb. As in the case of human mummies, a variety of procedures were employed, and the method described by Diodorus would have been one of the simplest. Scientific examination of cat mummies carried out in modern times has established the main stages of the process in some detail. The first step was optional. The corpse was opened, the internal organs removed and replaced with packing material, usually sand or mud, probably mixed with natron. It seems that the internal organs were not kept (those of people and, in exceptional circumstances, of some other animals such as Apis-bulls, were preserved in special containers which Egyptologists call 'canopic jars'). The cat's legs were then usually extended to fit neatly alongside the body which was stretched, treated with resin or similar materials, and tightly wrapped up in natron-soaked linen bandages. Reeds may have been used to provide some

105 A bronze cat mask, probably from Bubastis, c.664–30 BC. British Museum.

support for the mummified body. Sometimes the legs were left extended and bandaged separately so that the appearance of the mummified animal was more life-like. The combined effects of natron and a hot dry climate quickly took care of the rest. Temples with adjacent buildings where animals were kept must have had specialized staff for the mummification of animals and large establishments where it was performed as if on a conveyor belt.

The final preparation of the mummified body for burial varied from cemetery to cemetery; also, more than one method was used at each site. Most often it was felt to be sufficient to wrap the mummified cat in one or more layers of bandages and larger pieces of linen. These sometimes varied in colour and were made to form a decorative geometric pattern, usually lozenge-shaped or striped. Simple ornaments, such as a string of faience beads, may have been added. A mummified cat usually acquired a slightly tapering tubular form, with only the head with an imitation of the ears distinguishable. The shape of some other cat mummies is reminiscent of their human counterparts, with 'feet' and 'shoulders.' Facial features may have been painted on the bandages, or a bronze mask in the shape of a cat's head was sometimes placed over them. This was inspired by human burials; one of the best known ancient Egyptian monuments, Tutankhamun's gold mask, served the same purpose.

Sometimes the cat was put into a wooden coffin made up of a number of smaller pieces of wood. The coffin usually consisted of two adjoining halves and imitated the shape of the animal. Such a coffin may have been overlaid with gesso, with details such as collars and necklaces, similar to those found on bronze statuettes, painted round the animal's neck, or it could be gilded. This reflected the custom of burying people in anthropoid coffins which resembled that of a mummified body in shape, with only the head and occasionally the hands appearing from the wrappings. There are reports of bronze cat heads which were found fixed to such wooden coffins. Other coffins were miniature versions of the rectangular coffins with vaulted lids which we know from human burials. On the coffin, the person who was responsible for the cat's burial may be shown, his arms raised in adoration, in front of a cat.

Some bronze statuettes of cats which were manufactured hollow could be used to contain the remains of small cats. This procedure was common in the cases of smaller animals and birds but must have been an exception rather than the rule for cats; the majority of such statuettes are much too small to contain the remains of even very young cats. Other statuettes may have been attached to a small box which then contained the body of a mummified cat.

The large numbers of animals made it impossible to bury them in individual tombs and the chosen method depended on local conditions. The mummified

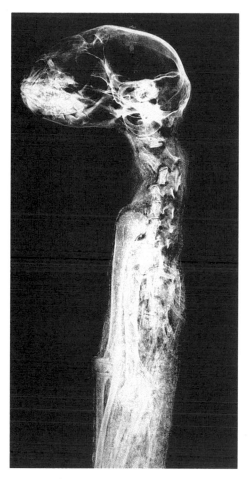

106 A radiograph of a cat mummy
showing the dislocated cervical vertebrae
which probably caused the animal's death.
London, The Natural History Museum.

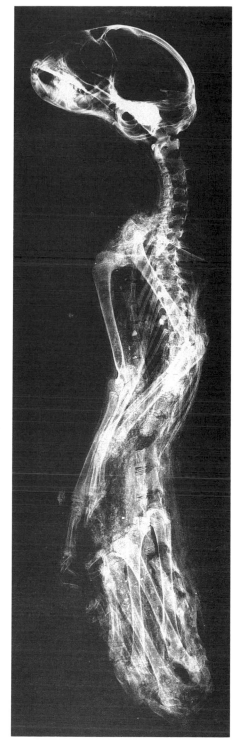

107 A radiograph showing the typical
position of the limbs of a mummified cat.
London, The Natural History Museum.

108 (*Above*) Three cat-shaped coffins made of gypsum-covered wood, with inlaid eyes. The piece in the centre demonstrates the method of manufacture in two halves, that on the right displays the remains of gilding. Probably Ptolemaic (332–30 BC) or even later. British Museum.

109 (*Left*) A small bronze casket with a feline figure, probably used to contain the remains of a cat, *c*.664–30 BC. British Museum.

cats may have been buried in communal brick-lined graves (Tell Basta), deposited in specially prepared rock-cut galleries (Dendera) or in re-used tombs of earlier dates (Saqqara), or placed in large pottery jars (Tell Basta, Abydos).

In view of what has been said about the fanatic zeal with which animals associated with deities were protected in late Egypt, it comes as something of a shock to discover that many of the mummified cats died young and some must have been hastened to their death. The numbers of animals examined are still relatively small, but from an investigation of cat mummies at the British Museum it appears that the majority of them died either at two to four months old, or between about nine and twelve months. The expected average age of a cat, reasonably well fed and looked after, should be some twelve years. A common cause of death was a dislocation of the cervical vertebrae, which would have happened if the head of the animal had been forcibly twisted and its neck broken. Others may have been strangled.

It has been suggested that these premature deaths were the result of a cull in a temple cattery which took place when the cats multiplied beyond what was acceptable. The theory seems reasonable and one can certainly see a need for such an occasion, however gruesome, arising from time to time if the numbers were allowed to grow unchecked, but other explanations are more plausible. Pilgrims who visited temples during annual religious festivals may have wished to pay for the mummification and burial of a cat as a visible expression of their piety. Deaths from natural causes would have been fairly evenly distributed throughout the calendar year, and so a certain degree of adroit but confidential management would have been required to ensure that pious Egyptians who wanted to display their religious fervour were not disappointed. The two age groups may have been selected because the size of very young animals would have been particularly suitable for the small

110 A bronze casket with the figures of two cats, one crouching, the other seated, from Saqqara, c.664–30 BC. British Museum.

containers in which they were buried, and in order to regulate the number of animals by reducing the number of male cats which reached sexual maturity (normally at some eight to fourteen months). This may seem like a rather cynical explanation but we know that, in spite of all their protestations to the contrary, the Egyptians could be remarkably unsentimental and level-headed people and such a solution, though not attractive, is not unthinkable.

An equally startling revelation is that many of the mummies are less than complete. Similar cases are known from the examination of human mummies from a later date where it is difficult to find an explanation other than that the body was damaged during mummification, either accidentally or due to the negligence of undertakers. It is possible that the same may have sometimes happened during the mummification of cats which almost certainly would have been done even less carefully and involved larger numbers of corpses. Sometimes, however, it seems that the incompleteness is such that it may have been intentional. It may be that these mummified animals reflect the changing attitudes towards the concept of mummification of human bodies discernible in Egypt in the Late and Ptolemaic periods. As if in recognition of the ultimate hopelessness of the task, the emphasis shifted towards the external appearance of the human mummy rather than the preservation techniques. The elaborate bandaging and the beautifully-decorated coffins and sarcophagi ensured that any defects would have been impossible to detect. Perhaps this make-believe approach was allowed to manifest itself more strongly in the mummification of animals, so that it was not always regarded as essential to preserve the body in its entirety. Maybe we should pause before scorning such curiously ambiguous and contradictory ways of thinking. Could they not be described as remarkably modern?

Epilogue

Our last words concern the fortunes of the cat following the demise of Egyptian pharaonic civilization and its Greco-Roman inheritors. The European wild cat (*Felis silvestris silvestris*), once common but now becoming extinct, has a reputation for being almost untameable. Egyptian domesticated cats probably reached ancient Greece from time to time and may be the rather ferocious-looking animals so much admired by Greek ladies on painted vases, perhaps as early as the fifth and fourth century BC. The much earlier, leonine-looking 'hieroglyphic' cats represented in appliqué relief on Minoan pots were contemporary with the later phase of the Egyptian Middle Kingdom, *c.*1875–1700 BC, but it is likely that the inspiration was artistic rather than from first-hand knowledge of the animal. The statement of Diodorus that Egyptians abroad ransomed captive cats and hawks in order to repatriate them to Egypt must be taken with a pinch of salt, but it was only in the early centuries AD that Egyptian cats spread to Italy in larger numbers (replacing and taking over the services of the ferret as a mouser) and then to the rest of the continent, to become our house cat (*Felis silvestris catus*). Some interbreeding with the indigenous wild cat is usually suggested.

Strangely, the cat did not bring with it its Egyptian name, but the new one poses a problem. In almost all European languages the word for the cat derives from the Latin *catus* or *cattus*, generally claimed to be first attested in the fourth century AD, although an earlier instance may exist. This is usually connected with *kadīs* in one of the Nubian dialects. Nubian cats may have been held in high regard, but such etymology appears strained and an intermediary of some kind, perhaps one of the North African languages, is probable. No better explanation, however, is available. In Arabic, the most common word for the cat is *qitt* or *qitta*. Attempts to link the word 'puss' or 'pussy' with the name of the Egyptian goddesses Pakhet or Bastet are certainly wrong. A connection, though not necessarily direct, with another Arabic word, *bass* or *bassa*, is probable but this can hardly claim an ancient Egyptian origin. In Upper Egypt, the word *biss* or *bissa* is applied to the wild (or feral) cat. Like the Romanian *pisică*, it may derive from the Turkish *pisi* and ultimately from the Persian *poshak*. The fact that in seventeenth-century English the word 'pussy' could also refer to the hare gives one some food for thought. The English 'tabby' derives from al-Atabiya, a quarter of Baghdad famous for the manufacture of striped silk taffeta to which the coat of tabby cats may be compared.

Between AD 639 and 642 Egypt was conquered by an Arab coalition led by Amr ibn al-As and became part of the Islamic world. Al-Qahira (Cairo) was founded in AD 969 and quickly became one of the greatest medieval cities of the world. Following the Ottoman conquest in AD 1520 the country's vitality seemed to have all but evaporated and its importance continued to decline until Napoleon's invasion in 1798 pushed it by force into the eagerly extended arms of the Western world. In 1922 its independence and a year

111 Two ladies with a pigeon and a cat, on a painted Campanian-style vase from Avella in Italy, 2nd half of the 4th century BC. British Museum.

later its constitution were at last proclaimed, and in 1952 it became a republic. At present, Egypt is trying to maintain a precarious balance between the rich West and its economic interests in the region, and the rising tide of Arab nationalism and religious fundamentalism, while at the same time tackling the enormous economic and human problems facing its people.

The cat, on the whole, has fared well. The Egyptians, whether Muslims or Copts, are fond of cats and mostly treat them kindly. Islamic religion displays considerable tolerance towards them. The Prophet Muhammad is said to have cut off a sleeve of his cloak so that he would not disturb a cat which had fallen asleep on it, and the streaks on the fur of the Egyptian cat are described as the marks left where the Prophet's hand stroked it. There are records of medieval donations to provide for the food for homeless strays of Cairo, some of which still existed in the last century. The best-known of such charities is perhaps that of the Sultan Baibars (AD 1260–1277) whose emblem was one of the big cats, and who left a garden near his mosque for the upkeep of destitute Cairo cats.

When entering a Cairo mosque, you can be sure that there will be a cat quietly sleeping somewhere in a corner of the courtyard, clearly feeling safe and very much at home. Life in modern Egypt is quite hard for ordinary people, and much more so for their animals. Of all the domestic animals, the cat has probably had the best deal. It may have been shorn of its divine connections, but when compared with the ancient Egyptian cat, its way of life probably did not change all that much in the Middle Ages and for many of them it still continues in the same way, little affected by 'progress,' in modern times. This, unfortunately, is in marked contrast to what we know about the barbaric treatment of cats in 'enlightened' medieval Europe, sur-passed only by the behaviour of people towards each other then, in more recent times, and in parts of the continent even now.

It may be that the welfare of animals and concern about their basic rights are luxuries which people in certain areas of the world can ill afford. More often than not, even those who can regard it as a sacrifice which they are not prepared to make. It is a depressing thought, and one cannot help feeling that the symbiotic relationship into which the cats and humankind entered voluntarily in Egyptian villages some 6000 years ago, has been betrayed by one of the parties to the contract.

Selected bibliography

Abou-Ghazi, D., 'Die Katze in Religion und Leben im alten Ägypten.' In: *Das Altertum*, 9 (1963): 7–16.

Alliot, M., 'Les auxiliaires de chasse du tueur d'oiseaux au bâton de jet.' In: *Bulletin de la Société Française d'Égyptologie*, 6 (1951): 17–25.

Altenmüller, H., *Die Apotropaia und die Götter Mittelägyptens. Eine typologische und religionsgeschichtliche Untersuchung der sogenannten 'Zaubermesser' des Mittleren Reichs*. München. 1965.

Anderson, J. and de Winton, W.E., *Zoology of Egypt: Mammalia*. London: Hugh Rees, Ltd. 1902.

Arkell, A.J. 'An early pet cat.' In: *Journal of Egyptian Archaeology*, 48 (1962): 158.

Armitage, P.L. and Clutton-Brock J., 'A radiological and histological investigation into the mummification of cats from ancient Egypt.' In: *Journal of Archaeological Science*, 8 (1981): 185–96.

Boessneck, J., *Die Tierwelt des Alten Ägypten, untersucht anhand kulturgeschichtlicher und zoologischer Quellen*. München: Verlag C.H. Beck. 1988.

Bonnet, H., *Reallexikon der ägyptischen Religionsgeschichte*, s.v. 'Katze.' Berlin: Walter De Gruyter & Co. 1952.

Brunner-Traut, E., *Altägyptische Tiergeschichte und Fabel. Gestalt und Strahlkraft*. Darmstadt: Wissenschaftliche Buchgesellschaft. 1968.

Clutton-Brock, J., *Domesticated Animals from Early Times*. London: British Museum (Natural History) and Heinemann. 1981.

Clutton-Brock, J. *The British Museum Book of Cats Ancient and Modern*. London: British Museum Publications and British Museum (Natural History). 1988.

Les Chats des Pharaons. '4000 ans de divinité féline.' Exposition, etc. Catalogue, 27 octobre 1989 – 25 février 1990. Bruxelles: Institut Royal des Sciences.

Delvaux, L. and Warmenbol, E., *Les Divins chats d'Égypte: un air subtil, un dangereux parfum*. Leuven: Éditions Peeters. 1991.

Hermann, A., 'Die Katze im Fenster über der Tür.' In: *Zeitschrift für ägyptische Sprache und Altertumskunde*, 73 (1937): 68–74.

Hopfner, T., *Der Tierkult der alten Ägypter nach den griechisch-römischen Berichten und den wichtigeren Denkmälern*. In: *Denkschriften der kaiserlichen Akademie der Wissenschaften in Wien, phil.-hist. Kl. 57* [2]. Wien: Alfred Hölder. 1913.

Hornung, E., 'Die Bedeutung des Tieres im alten Ägypten.' In: *Studium Generale*, 20[2] (1967): 69–84.

Janssen, R. and J., *Egyptian Household Animals*. Princes Risborough, Aylesbury: Shire Publications Ltd. 1989.

Keller, O., *Die antieke Tierwelt*, i. Leipzig: Verlag von Wilhelm Engelmann. 1909.

Kessler, D., *Die heiligen Tiere und der König*, i. *Beiträge zu Organisation, Kult und Theologie der spätzeitlichen Tierfriedhöfe*. Wiesbaden: Otto Harrassowitz. 1989.

Langton, N. and B., *The Cat in Ancient Egypt*. Cambridge University Press. 1940.

Lortet, L. and Gaillard C., *La Faune momifiée de l'ancienne Égypte*. Lyon: Henri Georg, Éditeur. 1905.

Malek, J., 'Ashmolean cats.' In: *The Ashmolean*, 8 (Autumn 1985): 12–16.

Malek, J., 'Adoration of the Great Cat.' In: *The EES Newsletter*, 6 (October 1990): 6–9.

Morant, H. de, 'Le chat dans l'art égyptien.' In: *Chronique d'Égypte* 12 (1937): 29–40.

Morrison-Scott, T.C.S., 'The mummified cats of ancient Egypt.' In: *Proceedings of the Zoological Society of London*, 121 (1951–2): 861–7.

Riefstahl, E., 'A sacred cat.' In: *The Brooklyn Museum Bulletin*, xiii [2] (Winter 1952): 1–15.

Robinson, R., 'Cat.' In: Mason, I. L. (ed.), *Evolution of Domesticated Animals*. London and New York: Longman. 1984.

Roeder, G., *Ägyptische Bronzefiguren*. Berlin: Staatliche Museen. 1956.

Scott, N.E., 'The cat of Bastet.' In: *The Metropolitan Museum of Art Bulletin*, xvii [1] (Summer 1958): 1–7.

Serpell, J.A., 'The domestication and history of the cat.' In: Turner, D.C. and P. Bateson, *The Domestic Cat: the Biology of its Behaviour*. Cambridge University Press. 1988.

Störk, L., 'Katze.' In: Helck, W. and W. Westendorf, *Lexikon der Ägyptologie*, iii. Wiesbaden: Otto Harrassowitz. 1980.

Tabor, R., *Cats. The Rise of the Cat*. BBC Books. 1991.

te Velde, H., 'A few remarks upon the religious significance of animals in ancient Egypt.' In: *Numen*, xxvii (1980): 76–82.

te Velde, H., 'The cat as sacred animal of the goddess Mut.' In: *Studies in Egyptian Religion dedicated to Professor Jan Zandee*. Leiden. 1982.

Yoyotte, J., 'Des lions et des chats. Contribution à la prosopographie de l'époque libyenne.' In: *Revue d'Égyptologie*, 39 (1988): 155–78.

Zeuner, F.E., *A History of Domesticated Animals*. London: Hutchinson. 1963.

Illustration acknowledgements

Frontispiece,

1, 2 BM 64391. H. 42cm.

3, 4 C. M. Johns

   5 BM 37976. H. 58.5cm

   6 BM 37978. H. 71cm

7, 8 Graham Harrison, from T. G. H. James, *Egypt the Living Past*, 1992, figs. 8,14

   9 Werner Forman Archive / Werner Forman

 10 Cairo, Egyptian Museum, JE 56601, photo Werner Forman Archive. H. 102cm

 11 © Roger Tabor

 12 Bruce Coleman Ltd. / D. & R. Sullivan

 13 BM 41842. H. 6.5cm.

 14 From Nina de Garis Davies and A. H. Gardiner, *The Tomb of Huy*, 1926, pl. xxviii.

 15 © Oxford Scientific Films / Eyal Bartov

 16 © John G. Ross

 17 From R. Macramallah, *Le Mastaba d'Idout*, Cairo, 1935, frontispiece

 18 Bruce Coleman Ltd. / Francisco Marquez

 19 From P. E. Newberry, *Beni Hasan*, i, 1893, pl. xxxiv

 20 Copy by Howard Carter, from F. Ll. Griffith (ed.), *Beni Hasan*, iv, 1900, pl. v

 21 Vatican, Museo Gregoriano Egizio, 22765. H. 56cm

 22 Hervé Champollion

 23 Photo Claudio Emmer, © Editions d'Art Albert SKIRA, Geneva

 24 From F. Cailliaud, *Recherches sur les arts et métiers*, 1831, pl. 37

25 New York, Metropolitan Museum of Art, 15.3.1708. H. 34.5cm. All Rights Reserved

26 Griffith Institute, Ashmolean Museum, Oxford. Gunn MSS. xiv.48(2). H. 55cm

27 From P. E. Newberry, *Beni Hasan*, ii, 1893, pl. vi

28 London, Petrie Museum, 14323. H. 30.5cm. Copied by the author, drawn by M. E. Cox

29 New York, Metropolitan Museum of Art. Purchase, Lila Acheson Wallace Gift, 1990 (1990.59.1). H. 11.4cm. All Rights Reserved

30 BM 24405. H. 6cm.

31 BM 57699-700. H. 1.2cm

32 Egyptian Expedition of The Metropolitan Museum of Art, New York, Rogers Fund, 1930 (30.4.411). All Rights Reserved

33 Drawing by Norman de Garis Davies. Griffith Institute, Ashmolean Museum, Oxford, photo. 1457

34 Painting by Nina de Garis Davies. Copy of a wall painting from the tomb of Anen (TT 120) (MMA 33.8.8). All Rights Reserved

35 Drawing by Norman de Garis Davies. Griffith Institute, Ashmolean Museum, Oxford, photo. 1456

36 Painting by Nina de Garis Davies. Copy of a wall painting from the tomb of Two Sculptors (TT 181) (MMA 30.4.105). New York, Metropolitan Museum of Art. All Rights Reserved

37 From Nina M. Davies and A. H. Gardiner, *Ancient Egyptian Paintings*, ii, 1936, pl. xcv

38 Painting by Norman de Garis Davies. Oxford, Ashmolean Museum, 1947.72

39 Painting by Norman de Garis Davies. Oxford, Ashmolean Museum, 1947.42

40 Florence, Museo Archeologico, 2525. H. 14.5cm

41 The Bodleian Library, Oxford, MS

Gardner Wilkinson, section B.II.9, fol. 18v (right)

42, 43 BM 37977. H. 81cm

44 Leiden, Rijksmuseum van Oudheden, AP.6. H. of the cat 9cm. Photo P. J. Bomhof, © Rijksmuseum van Oudheden

45 BM 32733. H. 22.2cm.

46 BM 24425 verso, drawing by Chris Barrett. L. 25.4cm.

47 BM 22900

48 BM 22941

49 John G. Ross

50 Griffith Institute, Ashmolean Museum, Oxford, photo. TAA 1296

51 BM 10470/10

52 BM 9901/8

53 The Bodleian Library, University of Oxford, MS Egypt a 4 (P) section A/4

54 From T. Säve-Söderbergh, *Four Eighteenth Dynasty Tombs*, 1957, pl. lvi (right). Reproduced with the permission of the Griffith Institute, Ashmolean Museum, Oxford

55 Arpag Mekhitarian

56 Oxford, Ashmolean Museum, 1961.232. H. 21.2cm

57 Turin, Museo Egizio, 50056. H. 14.2cm

58 Turin, Museo Egizio, 50053. H. 16cm

59 BM 48703. W. 0.9cm

60 The Brooklyn Museum, 16.41. H. of this fragment 10cm

61 BM 32747. H. 25.4cm

62 BM 63516. H. 26.7cm

63 BM 47547. H. 16.7cm

64 BM 58517. H. 16.5cm

65 BM 22927. H. 8.2cm

66 BM 11578. H. 3.8cm

67 BM 6768. H. 47cm

68 BM 11560. H. 20.7cm

69 BM 43045. H. 4.6cm

70 BM 25565. H. 26cm

71 BM 12590. H. 16cm

72 BM 36108. H. 7.2cm

73 BM 11031. H. 10.8cm

74 BM 57278. H. 18.9cm

75 Hildesheim, Pelizaeus-Museum, 748. H. 47cm

76 BM 38177. H. 15.4cm

77 BM 64558. H. 22.3cm

78 BM 60235. H. 7.5cm

79 BM 11236. H. 4.8cm

80 BM 60400. H. 1.9cm.

81 BM 27725. H. 8.3cm

82 BM 24749. H. 3.7cm

83 BM 61594. H. 2.7cm

84 BM 61591. H. 2.5cm

85 BM 11893. H. 4.4cm

86 BM 11543. H. 11.8cm

87 BM 61556. W. 11.5cm

88 The Brooklyn Museum, 37.51E. H. 8.9cm

89 The Oriental Institute, University of Chicago, 13951. H. 7.8cm. Photo. Jean M. Grant

90 Cairo, Egyptian Museum, JE 65429. Photo. © John G. Ross

91 Hildesheim, Pelizaeus-Museum, 3989. H. 12cm

92 The Fitzwilliam Museum, University of Cambridge, EGA.3859.1943. Photo. © Fitzwilliam Museum. H. 11cm

93 Brussels, Musées Royaux d'Art et d'Histoire, E. 6727. H. 9cm

94, 95 Drawings by Richard Parkinson after papyrus 55001 (details), in Turin, Museo Egizio

96, 98 BM 10016

97 Musée du Louvre, E. 17339, photo © R.M.N. — R. G. Ojeda

99 Drawing (partly reconstructed) by Richard Parkinson of a detail of papyrus in Cairo, Egyptian Museum, JE 31199

100 Copenhagen, Ny Carlsberg Glyptotek, ÆIN 449. H. 17cm

101 Cairo, Egyptian Museum, CG 50053. H. 64cm

102 BM 55409. H. 43.2cm

103 BM 37348. H. 45.7cm

104 BM 11562. H. 9cm

105 BM 11555. H. 6.3cm

106, 107 London, The Natural History Museum

108 BM 20725, 6761, 25299. H. 51.5cm, 52cm, 37cm

109 BM 6767. H. 2.5 + 3.2cm

110 BM 22540. H. 15.2cm

111 BM F 207 (Dept. of Greek and Roman Antiquities). H. 46.2cm

Index

Figure numbers are in **bold**